Shoetopia: Contemporary Footwear

Sue Huey & Kathryn Kenny

Laurence King Publishing Ltd

LAURENCE KING

Published in 2014 by
Laurence King Publishing Ltd
361–373 City Road
London EC1V 1LR
Tel: +44 20 7841 6900
Fax: +44 20 7841 6910
email: enquiries@laurenceking.com
www.laurenceking.com

A catalogue record for this book is available from the
British Library.

ISBN: 978 1 78067 345 5

Design: Eleanor Ridsdale
Additional picture research by Amanda Russell

Printed in China

Front cover: courtesy Daniele Michetti
Back cover: courtesy Aperlaï

Contents

Shoetopia

designers

in their

own words

Pared down

Intellectual

Contradicting textures

Sophisticated

Nostalgic

Romantic

Colourful

Fun!

Fetish

Fierce

Distinctive

Sensual

Sharp

Feminine

Subtle

Muted

Solid

Visionary

Utilitarian

Frivolous

Humorous

Expressive

Playful

Vibrant

Storytelling colours

Modern

Architectural

Eclectic

Textural

Familiar

Introduction

Since *New Shoes* was published in 2007, the appetite for footwear in all its guises has not waned. On the contrary, footwear has continued its rise up the fashion ranks to become the leading focus in the ever-evolving world of style. The avid interest in new design, alongside classic design, shows no sign of abating. Shoes are more prominent than ever before and, to celebrate this fact, we have hand-picked 40 of the most innovative and inspirational footwear designers and brands to feature in this book.

From established fashion houses to rising stars and emerging talent, each designer and brand interviewed and featured here has a different approach to design. And in researching and collating this book we have been lucky enough to delve into the minds and inspiration of these 40. From Parisian houses established since the 1800s to new designers and their debut collections, what is so compelling is that each brings a fresh approach to footwear design.

Within this book we explore the different journeys that each designer and brand takes when embarking on a new collection, and most importantly the kind of woman they have in mind when putting pencil to paper. The different approaches are fascinating; for each designer we met the journey is a unique one.

While designers continue to embrace traditional methods of craftsmanship, there is a definite shift towards the exploration of new techniques in shoe design. Silhouettes have taken on a more structural aesthetic, resulting in shoes that are wearable works of art. Think back to the surrealist times of Schiaparelli and you'll be able to draw a visible line to the designs of Charlotte Olympia and Minna Parikka. Designers such as Nicholas Kirkwood, Julia Lundsten of FINSK and Anastasia Radevich have become pioneers in the drive towards conceptual design, making it more acceptable within both high-end and mainstream fashion. Consumer attitudes are also changing, allowing designers to explore new possibilities in footwear and be more daring with their offerings.

Pink and turquoise *Pfeiffer*, from the Minna Parikka spring/ summer 2013 look book.

'Dreamfall' collection by Anastasia Radevich, spring/ summer 2011.

Jill, from the Alexander Wang
resort 2013 look book.

Whether used all over or as an accent, colour plays a hugely important role
in this new wave of modern footwear design. Material innovation is also key,
including degradé python, rubberized leathers and sueded alligator skins. The
synthetic and leather industries are continually developing new materials.

While structure, colour and material make up the essential elements of footwear
design, the underlying theme that keeps every designer alive is the woman
who will wear the shoe and ultimately make it her own. Many designers have
a definitive woman in mind when designing; Liam Fahy names his shoes after
the women who inspired them. Others, such as Alexander Wang, prefer the
character to develop organically, and then ask what makes that person feel
like an Alexander Wang girl. The factor that unites them all is the desire to
evoke emotion with their shoes, whether it be humour, a sense of seduction or
empowerment. All strive to enrich the lives of those who wear them.

Established brands such as Chanel, Prada and Louis Vuitton continue to
inspire each generation of young designers. While these core brands stay true
to their heritage, it is their ability to create innovative footwear season after
season that keeps them at the forefront of fashion. However, what has been
most encouraging while researching this book is the wealth of new design talent
coming into the market. Since the publication of *New Shoes* there has been an
influx of new, incredibly talented labels, each one as individual as the next. From
Bionda Castana to Daniele Michetti, each designer takes a different approach
when creating their collections, and here we have showcased those distinctive
qualities indicative of their unique styles.

Style *294–47* by FINSK,
spring/summer 2013.

Paul Andrew

Asteria Two-tone suede evening boot in ultraviolet and black suede, fringed with delicate feathers along one side. With pointed toe, covered stiletto heel and back zip closure. Pre-fall 2013.

Having designed footwear for some of the world's most iconic fashion houses, British-born Paul Andrew decided to strike out alone with a spring/summer collection for 2013. His previous work with the likes of Alexander McQueen, Calvin Klein, Narciso Rodriguez and Donna Karan has allowed him to perfect his skills and hone his vision for his US-based eponymous brand.

What inspired you to get into footwear design?
I've been passionate about fashion and design for as long as I can remember. My mother loves fashion and has closets filled with stiletto heels; growing up I adored sitting in her shoe closets studying the details. One particular pair I'll never forget were some flame-red pull-on boots in butter-soft calfskin, which inspired a boot in my first fall collection.

Do you have a particular kind of woman in mind when you are designing?
I try not to think of a single, specific woman when I'm designing as I love the idea that my shoes could be desirable to a number of different women.

Where do you draw your inspiration from?
I find that inspiration can come from anywhere and everywhere, whether that be art, design or nature – you just need to seek it out. That said, I've always enjoyed watching films from the 1930s and 40s, which has fostered a particular fondness for Ingrid Bergman, Gene Tierney and especially Marlene Dietrich. *Shanghai Express*, directed in 1932 by Josef von Sternberg, has had a significant influence on my current collections.

Would you say you had a signature style? Describe it to us in five words.
Elegant, chic, sensual, refined, comfortable (people in fashion are scared of this word, but it's my personal obsession to make my shoes comfortable).

When it comes to technique and fabric, are there particular styles and materials that run through each collection?
I develop most of my materials from scratch each season with the best tanneries and mills in Italy. This ensures exclusivity and freshness in the collection, but also allows me to develop an extremely high-quality product. A material I love to use is a triple-dyed suede that I developed with a very skilled Milanese tannery. In dyeing the suede repeatedly, the finished colour is extremely rich and saturated.

How do you see the current fascination with footwear developing?
A great pair of shoes can transform an outfit in more ways than any other accessory. Shoes are a kind of aesthetic punctuation, and like lipstick, they have the power to glamorize, feminize, empower.

What are your ambitions for your brand in the future?
The brand is still young and while I have many ideas for growth, I want to proceed steadily and responsibly. Outside of the clear objective to establish Paul Andrew as a signature force in the luxury women's footwear universe, in the coming years I would like to see freestanding boutiques in key fashion capitals, a men's collection and the elaboration of women's accessories into handbags.

1.

2.

4.

3.

1. *Pallida Soir* Chalk-coloured
   leather T-strap sandal
   with decorative turquoise
   beading and stiletto heel.
   Pre-spring 2014.

2. *Zenadia* White pointed-
   toe pump with scalloped
   edge and stiletto heel.
   Pre-spring 2014.

3. *Sahara* Royal-blue gladiator
   thong sandal with double-
   buckled ankle strap closure.
   Pre-spring 2014.

4. *Kimura* Silk striped jacquard
   and patent leather pump with
   scalloped edge and stiletto
   heel. Spring/summer 2014.

1.

4.

2.

3.

1. *Babylon* Yellow whipsnake and black patent leather cross-strap sandal with 10.5cm (4in) stiletto heel. Spring/summer 2014.

2. *Amazon* Black patent leather evening sandal with feathered ankle strap detailing. Spring/summer 2014.

3. *Europeaus* Yellow whipsnake stiletto sandal with fine delicate ankle strap. Spring/summer 2014.

4. *Europeaus* Black stiletto sandal in nappa leather with fine delicate ankle strap. Spring/summer 2014.

Aperlaï

Heralded as one of the most exciting names in footwear, Paris-based brand Aperlaï is fast becoming a celebrity favourite. Founded in 2009 by designer and former headhunter Alessandra Lanvin, Aperlaï's bold structures and eye-catching designs take their name from the ancient Lycian city, close to the designer's summer home.

Feminine and highly sophisticated, Lanvin's distinctive design style combines clean graphic lines with elements of deliberate contrast, such as mixing tiny, elegant ankle straps with oversized toe straps, and vice versa. Instead of using flashy decorative hardware, colour-blocking and flashes of vivid brights are used to accentuate the cut and silhouette of the shoe. Lanvin's love of exceptional materials is evident in her use of exotic skins such as python, ponyskin and stingray; other materials include velvet, mirrored metallics, glittered leather, mesh and transparent plastics.

Having studied Art History before embarking on footwear design, a love of modern art is an obvious point of reference for Lanvin's work. She cites Jackson Pollock as having inspired her material choices; for colour she looks to artists such as Picasso and Mondrian, while Welsh industrial designer Ross Lovegrove, renowned for his organic-inspired designs, informs her silhouettes and shapes.

Aperlaï's bold silhouettes and dynamic structures are indicative of its aesthetic. A perfect example of this is the solid 14cm (5½in) architectural 'Geisha' heel, first introduced for the fall/winter 2011/12 collection. Inspired by the Cubist period, it has now become one of the brand's most recognized shoe styles. The much-loved 'Gatsby' loafer, inspired by the type often worn by androgynous Hollywood star Katharine Hepburn, has also become a signature style and as such is updated every season in new materials and colour combinations.

The shoes are made near Venice by some of the finest craftsmen in Italy. Not only are they beautiful on the outside, but their interior is also produced with great love and attention. The French house consults with foot specialists on the tailoring of its soles, arches and heel heights to ensure maximum comfort and fit, regardless of style, which is perhaps another reason why so many covet its shoes.

Indeed Aperlaï's distinctive style has become synonymous with the world of celebrity and its red-carpet events. Gwyneth Paltrow, Naomi Watts, Ginnifer Goodwin and Amanda Seyfried are just some of the names who have fallen in love with the unique footwear brand that is guaranteed to offer something new and exciting every season.

Although relatively new to the footwear industry, Aperlaï has already carved a successful niche and has an ever-growing audience. Now available in over 20 countries worldwide, Aperlaï continues to grow. Influential retailers include the famous Dover Street Market and Harvey Nichols in London; Kirna Zabête and Saks 5th Avenue in New York; 10 Corso Como in Milan; Luisa via Roma in Florence; Tsum in Moscow; L'Eclaireur in Paris, and online fashion retailer shoescribe.com.

1.

4.

2.

1. *Catalan Bootie* A dramatic colour-blocked ankle bootie in fuchsia-pink and black suede with corset-style stud closure. Fall/winter 2012/2013.

2. *Straps Opaline* An ultra-feminine strappy sandal with leather lace back closure, in luxury snakeskin and nude leather. Spring/summer 2013.

3. *Geisha Doll* Mary Jane platform pump in Bordeaux velvet, with square toe and gold and black-flecked signature 'Geisha' heel. Fall/winter 2012/2013.

4. *Tris* Minimalist slingback pump with cutaway heel and transparent plastic inserts, in luxury nude-coloured nubuck leather. Spring/summer 2012.

3.

1.

4.

2.

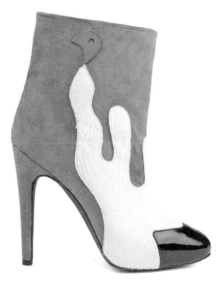

1. *Catalan* Showstopping
strappy sandal in patent
leather and suede with corset-
style stud back closure. Fall/
winter 2012.

2. *Birdie* Graphic ankle bootie
with patent leather toecap
and abstract appliqué in
suede and ponyskin. Fall/
winter 2012/2013.

3. *Demi* Bold and graphic,
this architecturally inspired
platform sandal features
the 'Geisha' heel. Spring/
summer 2013.

4. *Cat* Modern open-toe sandal
with decorative quarters and
back stud detailing, in luxury
snakeskin and suede. Spring/
summer 2013.

3.

Bionda Castana

Molly A cutaway pump with corsetry lace-up ankle strap detailing, in leopard-print ponyskin. Spring/summer 2012.

Showstopping, red-carpet glamour, ultra-feminine… these are all terms that could be used to describe Bionda Castana designs. However, the shoes behind the label are unique, and the secret to their originality and glamorous edge lies with the two designers who created the label: Jennifer Portman and Natalia Barbieri. The two half-Italian Londoners bring what is so great about each country to their designs. Fusing London's cool edginess with the craftsmanship associated with Italy, Bionda Castana's collections are completely irresistible to shoe lovers.

Established in 2007, Bionda Castana, named after the design duo's university nickname Blonde Brunette, is currently based in London but is on course for international expansion. Their collections fast became popular with the Hollywood glitterati, earning them coveted places on the feet of fashion-conscious stars Elizabeth Olsen and Keira Knightley.

Even among the sea of red-carpet luxe, Bionda Castana shoes stand out and steal the limelight with their unique designs and detailing, which have become a signature of the label. Sumptuous materials, normally associated with couture creations, are adapted and reworked to bring an air of opulence to the collection. Woven silks, lush velvets and the finest of leathers are mixed with studding and hardware to create distinctive styles.

Colour is also an important feature of the designers' aesthetic. Bold mixes such as ochre yellow with deep red on high-shine glacé kid leathers enhance the retro air of a vertiginous wedge pump. Elsewhere a simple suede slipper is given a regal punk twist with shocking pillar-box red colouring and zip edging.

These fun takes on classic designs, mixed with a daring use of colour, are what make the label stand out from the crowd.

Women are at the forefront of the brand's design ethos. Rather than simply creating works of art, Portman and Barbieri ensure that comfort is central to the design process. However thin the stiletto or towering the platform, the designers believe that 'looking good and feeling good are not mutually exclusive.'

Moving the brand forward and continuing to make an impact with their designs are what keep the designers delivering fresh collections. Although high-octane glamour is what they are currently known for, Bionda Castana believes in bringing a touch of their signature opulence to everyday wear too. Simple flat strappy sandals are given a new lease of life with luxurious leathers and embroidered fabrics, all in unusual but exotic colour combinations. Biker boots are given the Bionda Castana treatment with an intricate feminine approach shown through delicate studding and an elegant rounded toe. Covering the key shoes every woman needs in her wardrobe, Bionda Castana caters to its customers' needs, ensuring there is a style to accompany every look. It is a winning formula that has seen the design duo receive global recognition with the Best New Accessories Designer award at *Vogue Italia*'s Who is on Next event in 2008, only a year after their launch.

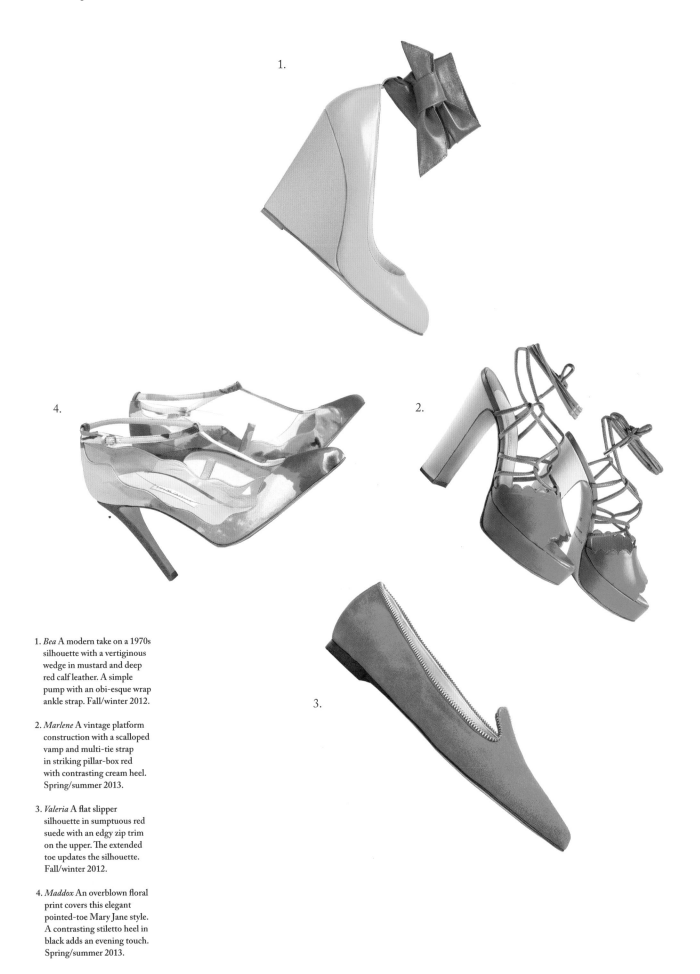

1.

4.

2.

3.

1. *Bea* A modern take on a 1970s silhouette with a vertiginous wedge in mustard and deep red calf leather. A simple pump with an obi-esque wrap ankle strap. Fall/winter 2012.

2. *Marlene* A vintage platform construction with a scalloped vamp and multi-tie strap in striking pillar-box red with contrasting cream heel. Spring/summer 2013.

3. *Valeria* A flat slipper silhouette in sumptuous red suede with an edgy zip trim on the upper. The extended toe updates the silhouette. Fall/winter 2012.

4. *Maddox* An overblown floral print covers this elegant pointed-toe Mary Jane style. A contrasting stiletto heel in black adds an evening touch. Spring/summer 2013.

1.

4.

2.

1. *Joan* A mix of floral silk, woven leather and clear plastic updates this platform sandal with ankle tie feature. Spring/summer 2013.

2. *Christa* Woven leather in cornflower blue features across this platform sandal. The style is made modern with a high-cut vamp and peep-toe upper. Spring/summer 2013.

3. *Elisabetta* In navy and nude, a modernist sandal featuring zip detail on the back of the heel. Spring/summer 2013.

4. *Maya* A geometric lace-up high-heeled sandal in Bordeaux suede with gold mini stud detailing. Fall/winter 2012.

3.

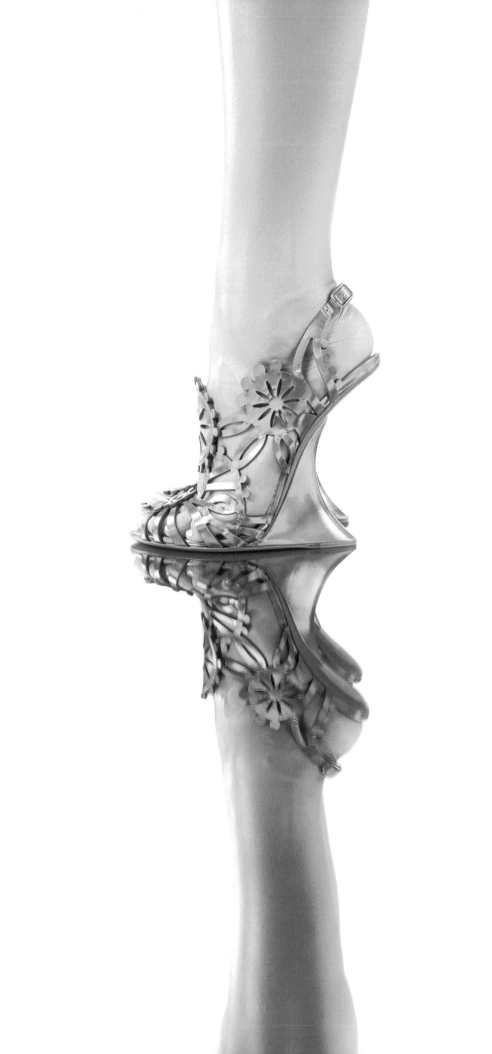

Edmundo Castillo

Reina An intricate laser-cut sandal in an iridescent gold mirror-effect leather, featuring a curvilinear wedge heel. Fall/ winter 2013/2014.

Puerto Rican designer Edmundo Castillo first ventured into the world of design as a teenager when he enrolled in the Altos de Chavón School of Design in the Dominican Republic. Upon graduation the budding designer moved to New York and embarked upon his love affair with footwear while working in various Manhattan shoe stores. Castillo's formal training in shoe design began at Donna Karan where he worked on the women's and men's footwear collections. After a brief one-year stint at Polo Ralph Lauren he returned to Donna Karan, designing the women's ranges for the main collection and for DKNY.

It was in 1999 that Castillo ventured to create his own line of women's shoes, launching in 2000. Only one year later he won the Perry Ellis Award for Best Emerging Accessories Designer from the Council of Fashion Designers of America. In 2004 Castillo put his collection on hold to become creative director of Italian fashion house Sergio Rossi, relaunching in 2010.

What inspired you to get into footwear design?
All of the women in my family. As a kid, I loved sneakers. At five years old I was already shopping for sneakers and shoes. But I grew up in a family with lots of women. Three sisters, nine aunts, dozens of female cousins – the shoe conversations during family gatherings were always very passionate.

Do you have a particular kind of woman in mind when you are designing?
When I think about the woman I design for, I like to think of her as modern and very self-confident about her style. And a shoe lover.

Where do you draw your inspiration from?
My inspiration comes from women, architecture, objects, art, colours, movies, books, life. Inspiration also sometimes comes from the least fashionable of things. But imagination can turn anything into a shoe.

Would you say you had a signature style? Describe it to us in five words.
Modern, simple, linear, sensual, timeless.

When it comes to technique and fabric, are there particular styles and materials that run through each collection?
I love colour. Materials that absorb colour beautifully, like suede or shiny calfskin, are always in the collection. I also love textures like snake or reptile, as well as the sleekness of patent leather and the shine of metallics.

How do you see the current fascination with footwear developing?
Shoes have always been very fascinating objects. Throughout the centuries shoes have been many shapes, lengths, widths and heights. Today, we are living in a very exciting time for shoes. There is new technology; there is so much room to play and create. But the joy that shoes give women is the same.

What are your ambitions for your brand in the future?
To shoe the world.

1.

4.

2.

1. *Tao* A pump gets a revamp
   in monochrome black
   and white. The contrast of
   patent and matt leathers
   adds modernity to the style.
   Spring/summer 2013.

2. *Tonya* An exotic upper in
   a monochrome colourway
   is applied to this futuristic
   construction. Oversized
   buckles enhance the graphic
   lines. Spring/summer 2011.

3. *Leah* A 1970s-inspired sandal
   in white glazed leather and
   mesh snake. An oversized
   oval buckle and chunky fluted
   heel emphasize the retro
   style. Spring/summer 2013.

4. *Patty* An oversized
   Edwardian-style buckle
   adorns this striking violet
   suede bootie with peep toe.
   Fall/winter 2012.

3.

1.

4.

2.

3.

1. *Temira* A gold leather ankle boot with curved stiletto heel. Thin straps overplayed onto gold mesh form the upper. Fall/winter 2013/2014.

2. *Vanessa* A vertiginous pump with a modernist platform. A laguna-blue suede strap sets off the snakeskin upper. Fall/winter 2012.

3. *Rosangela* An elegant evening sandal, updated in metallic snakeskin and gladiator-style straps. Spring/summer 2012.

4. *Eva* A fluted heel and platform sole give a vintage feel to this sandal in nubuck-finished snake with oversized buckle closure. Spring/summer 2012.

1. *Cha Cha* Sketch of a strappy platform mule in contrasting green and chocolate-brown leathers. The sculpted heel gives a modern twist. Spring/summer 2011.

2. *Naked Bootie* An elegant take on the gladiator sandal in camel calfskin leather with leather rope lacing. Spring/summer 2011.

3. *Debi d'Orsay* Stiletto-style evening shoe in animal print. Spring/summer 2011.

1.

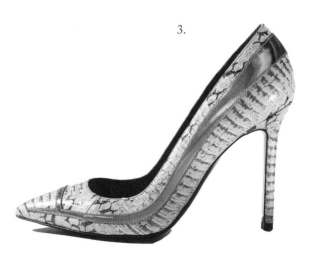

4.

2.

1. *Milla* A classic espadrille wedge updated in black and indigo. The multi-rope ankle strap has black chain looped through, bringing the style further up to date. Spring/summer 2011.

2. *Maravilla* A caged-effect cut-out stiletto sandal in a combination of taupe and gold suede. Fall/winter 2013/2014.

3. *Thelma* A pointed stiletto pump in fern-coloured wild snake with a flash of iridescent mirrored leather. Spring/summer 2013.

4. *Valerie* An exotic Swarovski-embellished sandal featuring a cut-out upper of wisps and curls in emerald-green crystals and violet-blue suede. Spring 2014.

3.

Chanel

Striped leather platform sandal worn with the women's ready-to-wear collection for spring/summer 2013, Paris Fashion Week runway show.

Iconic brand Chanel, founded in 1910 by Gabrielle Chanel, is synonymous with high-end luxury and unsurpassed quality and craftsmanship. Coveted and adored the world over, Chanel shoes bring joy and a sense of prestige to all who wear them. Well established in the world of footwear, Chanel is still one of the most aspirational brands today; its timeless elegance ensures that its shoes are always on the wish lists of footwear aficionados and collectors.

The legendary Chanel ballerina pump with its contrast toe and interlocking double 'C' logo in relief needs little introduction. A signature of the house, its timeless simplicity perfectly reflects the blend of elegance and restraint that Gabrielle Chanel set out to achieve.

Another key signature is the camellia motif. First introduced in the 1910s, Chanel's favourite flower has since been reinterpreted in new materials, colours, prints and finishes, and whether placed on the toe or on the side of the shoe is instantly recognizable as a symbol of Chanel luxury.

Since Karl Lagerfeld, head designer and creative director, joined the company in 1983, Chanel has continued to grow from strength to strength. While focusing on the Chanel dream Lagerfeld has rediscovered the brand's exceptional savoir faire and reinvigorated its heritage. He creates footwear styles that highlight all Gabrielle Chanel's original and elegant touches such as the spectator toe, gold accents, the camellia flower, quilting and chains, while at the same time adding his own artistic flair.

At Chanel, with luxury comes craftsmanship. Chanel's attention to detail is unsurpassed and in order to maintain its exceptionally high standards of quality,

it set up Paraffection in 2002. This Chanel subsidiary, made up of a collection of artisan workshops with whom Chanel has worked over the years, was created to help preserve dying artisan skills and encompasses such specialist areas as costume jewellery, feather making, millinery, embroidery, bootmaking, fabric-flower making, glove manufacturing and Chanel's shoe manufacturer, Massaro.

Founded in 1894 by the Massaro family, the prestigious footwear atelier is responsible for all the shoes ever made for Chanel, including its first and most iconic shoe, the two-tone slingback, created by Gabrielle Chanel in 1957. With its squared-off toe, beige upper to extend the leg, and contrasting black toecap to make the foot appear smaller, this slingback was designed primarily to prevent women getting grass stains on their shoes when they attended sporting events. The sleek silhouette was reissued in 2007 to celebrate its fiftieth anniversary and is one of 'les éléments éternels', as Karl Lagerfeld calls the brand's enduring signatures.

While the brand always holds true to its heritage, its ability to create innovative footwear styles every season has kept it at the forefront of fashion. From super-sleek thigh-high boots to chunky platforms, flatforms and androgynous lace-ups, the combination of Chanel's heritage and Lagerfeld's whimsical twist results in shoes that are both desirable and incredibly stylish. Chanel shoes are without doubt the ultimate investment in luxury footwear.

1.

4.

2.

1. Beige leather sandal with
   lighter-toned ankle strap and
   front detailing with stacked
   leather heel. Spring/summer
   2014 pre-collection.

2. Black leather pump with
   signature camellia flower
   appliqué. 2009/2010 Paris-
   Shanghai Métiers d'Art
   collection.

3. Espadrille and cork platform
   sandal with fine patent
   leather straps and subtle
   double 'C' logo. Spring/
   summer 2013.

4. Beige and black striped
   leather platform sandal,
   with cross-over ankle strap.
   Spring/summer 2013.

3.

1.

3.

2.

1. Black tweed and leather ankle bootie with faceted Lucite heel, crystal embellishment, fine-buckled ankle strap and logo. Fall/winter 2012/2013.

2. Black leather over-the-knee double boot with signature Chanel chain trim and block heel. Fall/winter 2013/2014.

3. Checked tweed and leather flat ankle boot with front zip closure and ankle strap detailing. 2012/2013 Paris–Edinburgh Métiers d'Art collection.

1.

4.

2.

1. Black leather sandal with
   coloured glass beads.
   2010/2011 Paris-Byzance
   Métiers d'Art collection.

2. Beige lace Mary Jane pump
   with pointed toe and lace-
   covered tapered heel. Cruise
   2014 collection.

3. Black and white tweed and
   patent leather ballerina,
   with interlocking double 'C'
   logo on the toe. Fall/winter
   2013/2014 pre-collection.

4. White leather loafer with
   signature chain trim and
   block heel. Fall/winter
   2013/2014.

3.

2.

1.

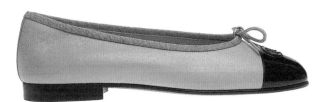

3.

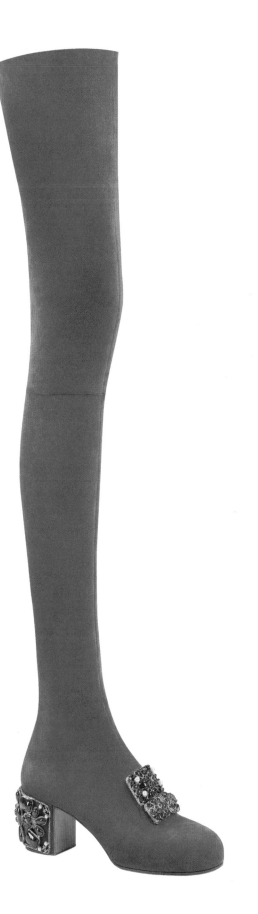

1. Beige and black signature
   two-tone ballerina shoe with
   tie detail. Spring/summer
   2014 pre-collection.

2. Burgundy suede high boot
   with cabochon detail.
   2010/2011 Paris-Byzance
   Métiers d'Art collection.

3. White and black two-tone
   pump with knotted rope heel.
   Cruise 2014 collection.

Jimmy Choo

Topaz A vertiginous wedge sandal in a striking colour combination of black and white with a strip of vivid green running down the back. Spring/summer 2012.

Catering for the woman who has everything but wants more, the Jimmy Choo label has become synonymous with luxury and power. The vertiginous stiletto heels and exaggerated silhouettes scream not only sex appeal but elegance too.

Jimmy Choo shoes are, quite simply, showstoppers. Patent leather infused with mesh inserts conjures up visions of 'behind closed doors' scenarios on a naughty-but-nice sandal, while a calf-length boot is adorned with luxurious fur in vibrant psychedelic hues. Smatterings of sequins, clusters of Swarovski gems, and rich embroideries are just some of the extravagant finishes you can expect from the brand.

There are classic Jimmy Choo styles too. The Italian craftsmanship is evident in the chic pointed toe and stiletto combination that fast became their signature style. Seasonally updated with new colour and fabric combinations, the staple court is a 'must have' for any Knightsbridge dweller.

The key to Jimmy Choo's success lies in its celebrity allure. The brand was one of the first to take its shoes and accessories to Hollywood, and the red carpet became the ideal catwalk to showcase its designs. The most high-profile feet, from style icons and celebrities to royalty, musicians and heads of state, have been spotted in its footwear. Its iconography was further defined by bold and dramatic advertising portraying glamorous but strong women in towering heels and luxurious handbags, captured by photographers such as Mario Testino, Terry Richardson and Steven Meisel.

The clever decision to take on Hollywood helped fuel the brand's rapid expansion. However, its roots can be traced back to much humbler origins. Begun by its namesake in the early 1990s, the bespoke shoemaker Jimmy Choo was based in London's East End where he was a graduate of the prestigious footwear college Cordwainers. Mr Choo was already catering for the global jet set with a glittering clientele including Diana, Princess of Wales. However it was in 1996, when Tamara Mellon, accessories editor at British *Vogue*, joined forces with him to found Jimmy Choo that the brand was truly established. Recognizing a niche in the luxury shoe market she started to build the empire that we know today.

With a goal of creating a global luxury business, Jimmy Choo attracted outside investment and the company embarked on a significant expansion across product categories, channels and geographies. Mr Choo left the company in 2001 and Mellon departed in 2011. Mr Choo's niece Sandra Choi is now sole creative director.

Cornering and ruling the niche luxury market has seen Jimmy Choo evolve into a lifestyle brand, with 140 stores in 32 countries. Women's shoes remain the core of the business with the addition of handbags, small leather goods, scarves, sunglasses, eyewear, belts, fragrance and men's shoes.

1. *Maury* This strappy sandal exudes opulence in a combination of red velvet and mirrored metallic leather. Zip fastening modernizes the style. Fall/winter 2012/2013.

2. *Maria* A modern-day gladiator in raw-edge natural tan and gold leather that reaches up to the ankle. The stiletto heel adds glamour. Pre-fall 2012.

3. *Teazer* lives up to its name in deep purple satin and a frivolous feather trim on the front. A slight platform adds a retro 1970s twist. Fall/winter 2012/2013.

4. *Kani* in a combination of supple nude suede and evening satin straps, which are encrusted with chunky Swarovski crystals. Pre-fall 2012.

1.

4.

2.

3.

1. *Glenys* Original sketch of an evening sandal with elegant multiple straps that create a cage-like effect. Secured at the front by a zip fastening. Fall/winter 2008/2009.

2. *Mary* Original sketch of a fun slip-on mule, which comprises two scarf-like straps. The red gingham fabric adds to the kitsch feel. Spring/summer 2001.

3. *Zaffira* Original sketch of a nude platform sandal encrusted in Swarovski jewels. The vertiginous heel is accompanied by a slight platform. Cruise 2011.

4. *Zap* Original sketch of an architecturally inspired sandal. The thin straps are reminiscent of a bridge construction; the colour blocking harks back to the Cubists. Spring/summer 2001.

1. *Tempest* A classic mix of silver
   sequins and black suede adds
   an evening sparkle to this
   strappy cut-out sandal. Fall/
   winter 2012.

2. *Gana* A peep-toe ankle boot
   in deep burgundy suede,
   featuring leather lacing
   woven into the upper to
   make a ethnic pattern detail.
   Pre-fall 2012.

3. *Taffy* A red sequinned Mary
   Jane style, with stiletto heel
   in complementary patent
   leather. Fall/winter 2012.

4. *Tasia* A deep-red burgundy
   suede platform sandal with
   sequin bow. Pre-fall 2012.

1.

2.

4.

3.

1. *Lance* Original sketch of a
   gold, curved line, cut-out
   sandal with stiletto heel.
   Cruise 2009.

2. *Feather* Original sketch of
   a simple evening sandal
   in silver. Delicate feathers
   adorn the front strap. Spring/
   summer 1998.

3. *Fringe* Original sketch of
   a knee-length stiletto boot
   with layered feather fringing
   and thong sandal detailing,
   creating an ethnic feel.
   Spring/summer 2002.

4. *Fleur* Original sketch of an
   elongated pointed-toe pump
   with extreme stiletto heel and
   black snake-print lace fabric
   upper. Fall/winter 2010.

Charline de Luca

Bourgeoise White multi-strap sandal with towering wedge sole featuring espadrille rope edging and cut-out detail.

Italian designer Charline de Luca could easily be called ' the new kid on the block'. Launching her first collection in early 2011, de Luca is most certainly one to watch in the world of shoe design. Like many of the most innovative designers in footwear today, her background did not originate in shoes but in architecture. Hailing from Rome, the place she credits for developing her 'taste for beauty and perfection', de Luca moved to New York to gain a BA in Architecture at the New York Institute of Technology. This is where her passion for footwear began and she decided to develop her love affair with shoes into a profession.

Determined to eventually launch her own successful and well-respected line, de Luca moved back to Rome in 2009 where she did a stint in the retail design department of major fashion house Fendi. It was a valuable experience that encouraged her determination to realize her dream. De Luca's next move was to follow in the footsteps of many of her contemporaries and enrol on a fashion course at the prestigious school of design, Central Saint Martins in London.

Now de Luca was ready and confident enough to create her first collection – and she has never looked back. She describes herself as a 'shoe architect', a title she lives up to with her sculptural signature style. Keeping to a minimal colour palette, which runs throughout her spring/summer 2013 collection, emphasizes this approach. Stark combinations of steel, pure white and black add depth to the clean lines and strategically cut strapping on her sandal uppers. The lines are often carried through on to the cut-out wedge sole, giving a futuristic optical-illusion effect to the design.

Materials that are more often associated with architecture and building are represented in her textural choices of fabric. Rough, natural hessians are teamed with glacé kid in metallic finishes. Exotic slices of stingray make up a blocked upper and are intertwined with plain, matt-white calf to create a combination that is startlingly modern. The designer describes the finished aesthetic as 'finding yourself in a world of shapes and geometries inspired by the work of architects and artists, like a homage paid to pure creativity.'

Staying true to this vision has been, and will continue to be, the key to de Luca's success and recognition in the footwear arena. In July 2012 she came third in Who is on Next, the international competition organized by *Vogue Italia* and Altaroma.

De Luca achieved artistic status when her 'Zaha' shoe (fall/winter 2012/13) was selected to be part of 'Shoe Obsession', an exhibition showcasing leading shoe designers at the Museum at the Fashion Institute of Technology in New York in 2013.

1.

2.

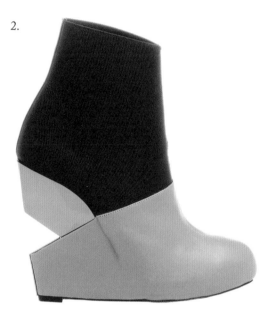

4.

1. *Leigh* Ankle bootie in matt
   mustard-yellow leather
   with bulbous toe shape and
   vertiginous wedge. Fall/
   winter 2013.

2. *Vreeland* Geometric ankle
   boot in matt leathers. A
   combination of neutral
   camel, black and grey with
   cut-out wedge detail. Fall/
   winter 2013.

3. *Lou Lou* Geometric ankle
   boot with pull-on neoprene
   sock feature. High block heel
   and upper in matt black and
   neutral beige leather. Fall/
   winter 2013.

4. *Kiki* High-cut slip-on shoe
   with concealed platform.
   The heel and ankle are
   highlighted in bright
   mustard. Fall/winter 2013.

3.

1. *Dumas* An elegant zigzag strappy sandal in a combination of red snakeskin and red matt leather with sculptural high heel. Spring/summer 2013.

2. *De Lempicka* Geometric strapping in monochrome snakeskin and matt black gives this cutaway wedge style a futuristic feel. Spring/summer 2013.

3. *Riley* A high platform sandal with wraparound snakeskin strap detailing that merges into the heel covering. Spring/summer 2013.

4. *Rego* A muted grey strappy sandal with high-contrast, wide red strap wrapped round the ankle, featuring simple closure detailing. Spring/summer 2013.

DKNY

DKNY

A simple pointed pump with asymmetric vamp detailing in leopard-print ponyskin. Fall/winter 2012.

No other brand quite embodies the spirit of New York like fashion designer Donna Karan through her label DKNY. Self-described as 'the energy and spirit of New York', DKNY is the younger sibling of the main Donna Karan collection launched by the designer and her late husband Stephan Weiss in 1984. DKNY itself was born in 1989 and was originally founded so the designer could dress her daughter Gabby, as well as venture into the world of denim.

When creating the brand, Karan set out to address the real-life needs of people everywhere. She thought about the collection in terms of a lifestyle idea, understanding that people on the street had a desire to look stylish in all aspects of their lives. And so she set out to create a global brand that could cover all of these needs. From 'work to weekend, jeans to evening', the DKNY label was fashionable as well as friendly… a girl's best friend.

The mantra of the seven-piece system that resonates throughout the Donna Karan line is directly applied to DKNY. The concept is that a woman's entire wardrobe can be built around just seven core pieces that when put together create a concise capsule wardrobe that will cover all eventualities, from office to bar and, more importantly, season to season.

Where other designers focus on creating a new collection every season, Karan recognizes that her customers' tastes and styles do not necessarily change with the fashion calendar. 'Everything I do is a matter of heart, body and soul,' says Karan, still chief designer of the international company that bears her name. 'For me, designing is an expression of who I am as a woman, with all the complications, feelings and emotions.'

This attitude touches all aspects of the label, and is not lost on the DKNY footwear collection. Practical, classic and stylish are all words that can be associated with the brand. Leopard-print materials (which continue to be in fashion season after season) can be found on a simple brogue, updated with a block heel. Concealed wedges add a streetwise touch to fashion trainers that have been given the luxe touch with intricately cut leather uppers.

Spring/summer 2013 saw the continuation of the sports luxe theme, a style which sums up the practical yet fashion-led aesthetic of the brand. Stealing the show was a strappy Velcro upper, given a new persona with the addition of a contrast-colour platform and pointed upper. The stiletto heel adds instant sex appeal and sensuality.

Donna Karan sums up her design approach, one that ensures her brand will continue to adorn the feet of the fashion elite for many years to come. 'That I'm a woman makes me want to nurture others, fulfil needs and solve problems. At the same time, the artist within me strives for beauty, both sensually and visually. So design is a constant challenge to balance comfort with luxe, the practical with the desirable.'

1.

2.

1. A futuristic take on a sneaker with stiletto heel and contrasting white platform. A pointed-toe upper in black calfskin and perforated leather features wide Velcro sports strapping. Spring 2013.

2. The combination of tactile ponyskin and smooth calf, all in black, gives a hard edge to this high bootie with rounded toe. Fall/winter 2012.

3. A high heel and concealed wedge version of the same style, in felted material with tonal suede trimmings on the toe and heel. Fall/winter 2012.

3.

1. Futuristic pointed sneaker style on high-heel construction. Runway, spring 2013.

1. Silver neoprene upper on cleated sole and with stiletto heel, with highlights of neon green and sports stitching detailing. Fall/winter 2012.

2. Behind the scenes at the spring/summer 2013 runway show, featuring gold and black high-heeled sneakers.

1.

2.

3. Embellished sneaker styles featuring intricate cutaway gold uppers, encrusted silver glitter uppers and a simple sneaker with metallic trim. Fall/winter 2012.

4. Behind the scenes shot at the spring/summer 2013 show; concealed-wedge sneakers in plain white and black and white.

3.

4.

LIAM FAHY

LONDON

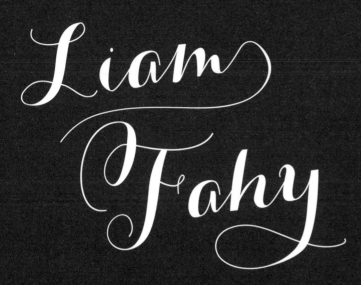

Liam Fahy

Underside view of the Liam Fahy signature metal logo, which is embedded in the soles of each pair of shoes.

Handmade in limited numbers, Liam Fahy's luxury artisanal designs are each embellished with a nickel sole signature. Fahy's rich and diverse background has greatly influenced his unique blend of footwear. Born in Zimbabwe to an Irish father and English mother, Fahy spent part of his childhood living on a snake farm and in his student years went to experience life with the Tonga tribe in the remote valleys of the Zambezi River.

After many years working alongside Rupert Sanderson, the brand launched its first collection in spring/summer 2012 after winning the first Fashion Fringe award 'chosen by the "Shoe-Father" himself, Manolo Blahnik'.

What inspired you to get into footwear design?
I grew up in Africa where I had to make most of my own things. After I made my first pair of traditional *Mbatata* sandals (which are made out of old truck tyres) at the age of about 14, I knew I wanted to design footwear.

Do you have a particular kind of woman in mind when you are designing?
Every shoe I design is named after the person who inspired it. Without some form of personification a design loses its context. The 'Briege' for example is named after my little sister, the 'Charlotte' after my girlfriend. It's giving a shoe a personality.

Where do you draw your inspiration from?
For me it is all about making women look and feel sexy; I love the psychology of fashion. I get much of my visual inspiration when I go home to Africa every year.

Would you say you had a signature style? Describe it to us in five words.
Scientifically engineered to be sexy (ha-ha). The 'Charlotte' is probably my signature design. It's based on a classic ballet shoe and has a hidden platform to make the shoe look like it's floating above the ground.

When it comes to technique and fabric, are there particular styles and materials that run through each collection?
My signature palette is quite dark and that does run though every collection. I love playing with different textures and types of black, although last season we went to Africa to find a vibrant Java print for the spring/summer 2013 'Congo' collection, and since then I've loved tribal prints.

How do you see the current fascination with footwear developing?
I think a new market of couture will emerge, similar to the world of art. It's something we can see already with our own shoes – they're more expensive than the average luxury shoe as our quality and standards are unsurpassed. We share the same heelmaker as Chanel and Givenchy, the same tanneries as Manolo Blahnik and Azzedine Alaïa, we even share the same box supplier as Christian Louboutin. There is certainly a developing market for super luxury.

What are your ambitions for your brand in the future?
I just want to make shoes, and make the women who wear them feel sexy.

1.

4.

2.

3.

1. *Charlotte* Tie-front platform pump, one of Liam Fahy's key styles in Java print with 10.5cm (4in) heel. Spring/summer 2013.

2. *Brigitte* Open-front sandal with ghillie lacing, back zip closure and 10.5cm (4in) stiletto heel in black vitello leather. Spring/summer 2013.

3. *Veva* Classic stiletto pump with toe seam detailing in red water-snakeskin with black contrast piping. Spring/summer 2013.

4. *Adora* Transparent mesh and suede peep-toe lace-up with silk ribbon laces and 10.5cm (4in) stiletto heel. Spring/summer 2013.

1.

4.

2.

3.

1. *Brigitte* Open-front sandal with ghillie lacing, back zip closure and 10.5cm (4in) stiletto heel in red water-snakeskin. Spring/summer 2013.

2. *Charlotte* Black lace stiletto platform pump with silk ribbon ties. Fall/winter 2013/2014.

3. *Lis* Sleek criss-cross strappy sandal with double buckle closure and stiletto heel in vitello leather. Spring/summer 2013.

4. *Alys* 11.5cm (4½in) wedge heel bootie with peep toe and side zip closure in zebra-print suede. Spring/summer 2013.

Feminine & Masculine

Dolores Bright A traditional-style lace-up in oxblood leather is modernized with a mesh insert on the upper. Spring/ summer 2013.

Mexican brand Feminine & Masculine, created by designer Francisco Rodriguez, originated in late 2008. California-born Rodriguez first trained in graphic design at The Art Institute of California in San Diego. His training in footwear began immediately after, when he moved to Barcelona, Spain to continue his studies, this time in shoe design and pattern making.

Rodriguez's passion for leather was sparked as a student in Spain when he started exploring new ways of treating leather and other materials to enhance and distinguish his designs from others. After applying these skills to clothing and accessories, Rodriguez turned his attention to more technical details. Structure and construction, alongside his exuberant use of clashing vibrant colours, are evident in his collections. All of these character traits, which Rodriguez has developed since his studies, make up the aesthetic of Feminine & Masculine.

Leather, in its different guises, is still pivotal to the Feminine & Masculine collection. From interesting finishes to the traditional humble cowhide, all are given a different personality. This is what makes his collection so innovative in footwear today.

What inspired you to get into footwear design?
The creativity behind a simple pair of shoes, the endless options for originality, the craftsmanship, the technical processes are what inspired me to design footwear.

Do you have a particular kind of woman in mind when you are designing?
The woman I have in mind when designing is able to embrace youth as a state of mind instead of a characteristic; she develops a style entirely based on the notion of personal freedom and individuality.

Where do you draw your inspiration from?
Mostly nature, but also everything and everyone around me.

Would you say you had a signature style? Describe it to us in five words.
Mixed, simple, bold, classical, technical.

When it comes to technique and fabric, are there particular styles and materials that run through each collection?
There is a way of doing things that is particular to us – mixing many components but always with a lot of handwork; not precisely crafty so much as crafted.

How do you see the current fascination with footwear developing?
I really think the recent hype in footwear comes from its versatility; women have options that are not only based on looks, but on practicality and needs. Their wishes will develop into styles that are both objects of desire and quality.

What are your ambitions for your brand in the future?
To increase Feminine & Masculine's presence in its established markets and to maintain its good quality and service; also to innovate and move forward.

1.

2.

3.

1. *Greta Noir* A contemporary take on the monk shoe in embossed crocodile leather and mesh fabric with EVA sports-style sole. Spring/summer 2013.

2. *Grace Noir* Peep-toe ankle boot in embossed crocodile leather with zip fastening, block heel and gold piping. Spring/summer 2013.

3. *Baxter Noir* Flatform sandal with multi-strap detailing. Glossy leather and mesh fabrication upper enhance the sports feel. Spring/summer 2013.

1.

2.

1. *Grace Pale* Peep-toe ankle
   boot in matt oxblood
   and olive leather with zip
   fastening. The block heel
   and bright red piping add
   a modern twist. Spring/
   summer 2013.

2. *Garbo Noir* A monk shoe
   construction in mesh fabric
   and leather trims, with EVA
   sports-style sole. Spring/
   summer 2013.

FINSK

Knee-high, pointed-toe boots with curved stiletto heel, in burnt bronze reflective leather.

FINSK was established in spring/summer 2005 by Finnish-born Julia Lundsten. Lundsten started working on her first collection while she was still a student at London's Royal College of Art, from where she graduated in 2003. The FINSK aesthetic, which draws heavily on Scandinavian furniture design, can be traced back to Lundsten's family roots; her parents worked in architecture and interior design. Design features and materials that are normally associated with furniture design form the basis of a FINSK shoe. Wooden heels and structural platforms are two of the features that make a FINSK shoe instantly recognizable.

What inspired you to get into footwear design?
I grew up with architect parents, and design was always a common topic at the dinner table. I then came to London to study womenswear initially, and gradually my interest in footwear evolved. I became fascinated with the more structural, architectural side of fashion – pattern cutting and shapes, as well as interesting materials.

Do you have a particular kind of woman in mind when you are designing?
An independent, modern woman who knows her style and isn't afraid to experiment. She understands about good-quality materials and has an eye for detail.

Where do you draw your inspiration from?
Nature; materials and their own interesting characteristics; architecture; animation and films; interesting people, places and cultures.

Would you say you had a signature style? Describe it to us in five words.
Modern, architectural, experimental yet wearable.

When it comes to technique and fabric, are there particular styles and materials that run through each collection?
I mostly favour traditional natural materials, such as leather and wood, as my style is so graphic and architectural. I like to use natural materials in contrast, creating modern pieces that are not aggressive, but organic and contemporary.

How do you see the current fascination with footwear developing?
Because shoe design has been in the spotlight, some of it has become a bit too much – crazy shoes just for the sake of it. I feel there needs to be a deeper thought behind outrageous designs, a reason why. I launched the FINSK Projects as a totally experimental division of our brand, where it's all about trying out shapes, colours and materials – not necessarily within the frames of 'good design' – and not being afraid to make mistakes. We show these shoes like showing sketches or prototypes of ideas before they are polished and finished. Through the experimentation I've come up with all kinds of new solutions that I apply to the main collections. I think designers need to keep pushing designs forward while remembering the woman who will wear the shoe, rather than just creating 'weird' footwear. Attention to luxury, high-quality materials, details and finishes will set designs apart.

What are your ambitions for your brand in the future?
To be able to keep the designs experimental without compromising aesthetics or ideas for commerciality. And to keep making our customers happy.

1.

2.

1. *N. 338-32* Block-toe pump
   with cut-out detailing. Soft
   matt-grey suede upper
   contrasts with geometric
   patchwork-covered block
   heel. Spring/summer 2013.

2. *N. 478-00* Matt and textural
   leathers, suede and varnished
   wood combine to give a
   tactile feel to this peep-toe
   shoe with geometric platform
   sole. Spring/summer 2013.

1.

2.

1. *Project 3* Geometric cut-out upper in ochre, grey and black with an extreme, conceptual wedge sole.

2. *N. 478-00A* A combination of matt and textural leathers and suede give a tactile feel to this peep-toe shoe with geometric platform sole. Spring/summer 2013.

1.

2.

3.

1. *116-34* A panelled gold snake peep-toe upper on a black suede platform sole with wooden layered conical heel. Fall/winter 2009/2010.

2. *N. 477-01* Sumptuous soft grey suede is gathered to create a pointed-toe upper. Geometric yellow and white demi wedge in EVA. Spring/summer 2013.

3. *116-08* A tactile grey fishskin upper on a wooden and leather-covered geometric heel and platform sole. Spring/summer 2009.

1.

3.

2.

1. *Project 2* A peep-toe upper in neutral beige fishskin is mounted onto a conceptual geometric cut-out platform covered in panels of glossy calfskin.

2. *252–43* A simple ankle boot is transformed with a two-tone suede upper and geometric cut-out wedge sole in a combination of grey, cobalt blue and natural wood. Fall/winter 2009/2010.

3. *153–11* Wood and raw-edge veg tan combine to create a modern take on the clog style. Spring/summer 2012.

Pedro García

Zadia Brown chunky stone Vachetta thong with stud detailing on the insole. From the spring/summer 2011 collection look book.

Dating back to 1925, Pedro García is today run by the third generation of the García family. Based in the Spanish shoemaking town of Elda, Alicante, Pedro García has always tried to ensure all of its output is manufactured within the town itself. This is just part of the brand's commitment to the 'Made in Spain' philosophy, which is also used as part of its logo.

Do you have a particular kind of woman in mind when you are designing?

There isn't a single Pedro García woman. They're all different from one another, and no doubt they all like to feel different too. But what I can say is that she's open-minded, versatile and receptive to new possibilities. And she's decisive: she knows what she wants, what she likes and what she's looking for. She likes design and fashion, she's interested in functionality, and she's looking for comfort.

Where do you draw your inspiration from?

Pedro García's collections are never based on a particular theme or inspiration, either as a starting point or as a guiding principle. They evolve in a natural way and one gives rise to the next; collections are sometimes even a revival and reworking of themes from seasons long past. This is because the brand's design approach is based to a large extent on experimentation, mainly with materials, but also with constructions and silhouettes. Sometimes we will take things out of context or put them in places they shouldn't be, with startling results.

When it comes to technique and fabric, are there particular styles and materials that run through each collection?

For Pedro García, it's essential to feel a special attraction towards the material you're working with, to understand it, to know the results you want to get, and to employ the right technique in order to achieve them. Some of our signature materials include silk, Swarovski crystal mesh and, most importantly, the anatomic insole. Whether hidden or visible, on flats or heels, with platforms or without, it has become one of the most recognizable elements in Pedro García's designs.

Would you say you had a signature style? Describe it to us in five words.

Experimental, bold, unique, easy and sincere.

How do you see the current fascination with footwear developing?

We welcome the new interest in shoes, but there's a risk of undervaluing the role of the professional shoe designer. Thinking that anyone who has the inclination and a bit of artistic ability can design a shoe is unfounded. There's a growing danger of trivializing the importance of professionalism in design.

What are your ambitions for your brand in the future?

Our aim is to strengthen and enhance the presence of the brand in the international market. Among our creative projects, we have recently started designing bags, and the plan is to continue diversifying into other product lines. The main objective is to position Pedro García as the leading Spanish footwear brand worldwide.

1. *Teri* H-vamp buckled
   comfort sandal in raw-edge
   leather with suede-covered
   wedge. Spring/summer 2011.

2. *Erika* Wooden platform clog
   pump in raw-edge beaver
   skin and wooden heel. Fall/
   winter 2012/2013.

1.

2.

1.

3.

2.

1. *Galatea* Fisherman thong in unlined raw-edge full-grain cowhide, with super-flex sole and antiqued buckles and studs. Spring/summer 2013.

2. *Mariel* Olive-green, raw-edge natural cowhide and natural python sandal with snap closure and 8.5cm (3½in) cigarette heel. Spring/summer 2013.

3. *Zulimar* Neon-yellow skinny crystal thong featuring cotton canvas straps with fine crystal embellishment. Spring/summer 2013.

1. *Belkis* Electric-blue deep
   V-cut bootie with rounded
   top-line in raw-edge suede
   and back Velcro strap closure.
   Spring/summer 2012.

2. *Beverly* Petunia peep-toe
   pump with oversized frayed
   floppy bow, 11cm (4⅜in)
   covered heel and forepart
   platform. Fall/winter
   2012/2013.

3. *Cheryl* Jewelled peep-toe
   platform sandal with cut
   stone decoration and Velcro
   closure. Spring/summer 2012.

1. Colour variations of the
   Charlize platform sandal in
   raw-edge beaver skin with
   anatomical platform and
   Velcro strap closures. Spring/
   summer 2012.

Pierre Hardy

Black multi-strap platform sandal with flashes of neon orange. Spring/summer 2009.

Say the name Pierre Hardy to any discerning fashionista and the first thought that will immediately spring to mind are his fantastical, structural footwear collaborations with Balenciaga. The Parisian designer joined forces with Nicolas Ghesquière in 2001 and has since gone on to create some of the most inspirational shoes in the fashion house's history.

Hardy's background includes collaborations with the crème de la crème of French design houses. He started his footwear career designing for Christian Dior and went on to be named creative director of the women's, then men's, footwear collections at Hermès in 1990. This paved the way for Hardy's launching of his eponymous collection of women's shoes for spring 1999. In 2002 and 2006 respectively, he followed it up with a men's collection and a new bag line.

Hardy's shoes are instantly recognizable. His passion for fine arts and architecture is visible through the clean lines and graphic silhouettes that have become his signature. His focus is squarely on the construction and design of the object as he rigorously works through the strengths of an idea, developing logical formulas and solutions. The results are creations that push silhouettes to the extreme while maintaining a sense of proportion and wearability; no mean feat.

Within his women's collections, Hardy tends to favour classic materials of kid, patent and box-calf leathers and satin touches – enforcing his dedication to a clean graphic line. He keeps his colours to a minimal palette of black and white, with slices and dashes of primary brights. Embellishment is minimal. Buckles are exaggerated into Cubist forms, a seemingly simple peep-toe pump is transformed with horizontal striped leather, while towering wedges take on a life of their own in rainbow-bright patchwork.

When you buy a Pierre Hardy shoe, you buy a piece of the designer himself. Nothing says this more than the first boutique he opened in Paris in 2003. A true reflection of his unwavering aesthetic, the designer says he 'dreamt up a small boutique like a monochrome jewel-box, with satiny floors of waxed black linoleum, a matt ceiling, and walls in reflective fabrics that add to the intimacy of the space.' Hardy's empire continues to grow. February 2009 saw the opening of a second store, on Paris's left bank, while in December 2010 he opened his first American Pierre Hardy flagship in New York's West Village.

What is most inspiring about Hardy is his constant challenge of what is feminine and sexy. He stays true to his vision with every creation, resulting in a strong style that is equal parts graphic and sensual. In essence, the woman who wears a Pierre Hardy shoe is not afraid to make a statement. In fact she encourages it.

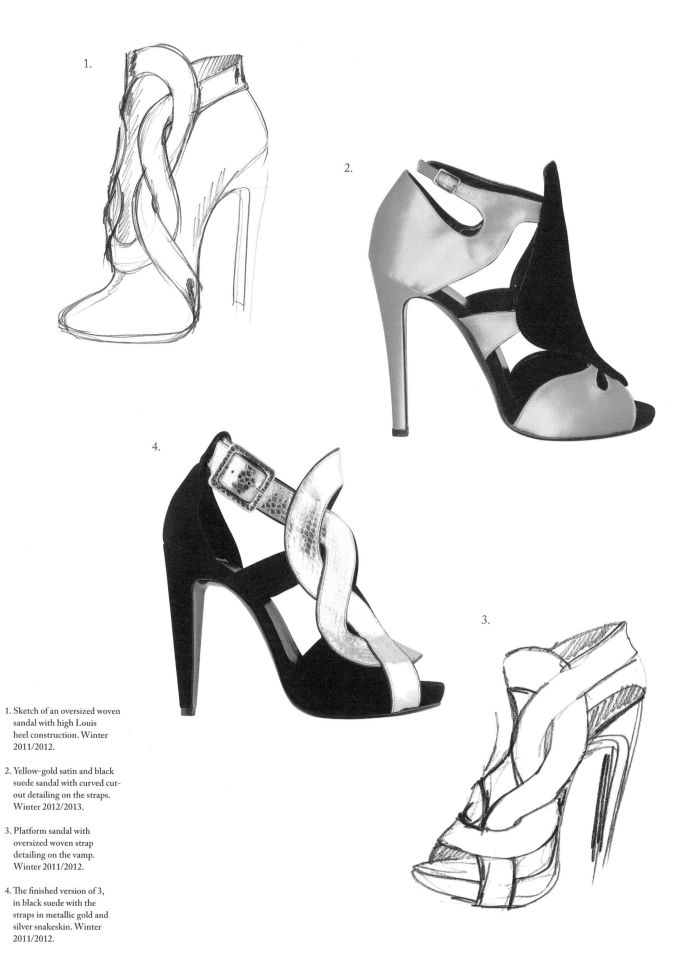

1. Sketch of an oversized woven
   sandal with high Louis
   heel construction. Winter
   2011/2012.

2. Yellow-gold satin and black
   suede sandal with curved cut-
   out detailing on the straps.
   Winter 2012/2013.

3. Platform sandal with
   oversized woven strap
   detailing on the vamp.
   Winter 2011/2012.

4. The finished version of 3,
   in black suede with the
   straps in metallic gold and
   silver snakeskin. Winter
   2011/2012.

1.

4.

2.

1. Striped peep-toe pump in a buttersoft nappa leather. The striking camel and cream colourway covers the whole upper as well as the heel. Summer 2006.

2. Extreme pointed slip-on shoe in black and white watersnake pattern. The web lacing on the upper adds a sporty edge to the stiletto shoe. Winter 2012/2013.

3. Circular 'peacock' feathers form the upper of this high-heeled platform sandal. Winter 2010/2011.

4. Exaggerated spiky cut-outs surround the ankle of this strappy sandal/pump hybrid. Metallic leathers and spray paint-effect leathers heighten the drama of the style. Winter 2008/2009.

3.

1.

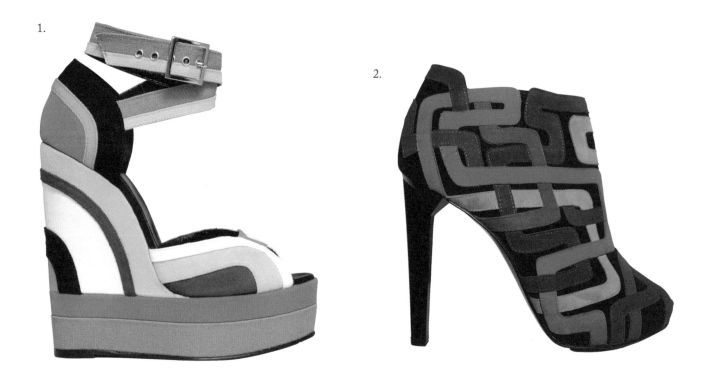

2.

3.

1. A truly retro wedge style in a riotous colour combination of turquoise, red, white, black and pink appliquéd fabric. Summer 2012.

2. Geometric lines of bright red, navy and turquoise suede are appliquéd onto a black peep-toe bootie. Winter 2012/2013.

3. An espadrille sole is modernized with an extreme geometric upper in patent leather with black suede straps. The glossiness of the red provides a perfect contrast between traditional and modern. Summer 2011.

1.

2.

3.

1. A black satin sandal is transformed with a blue footbed and red geometric adornment on the ankle. Winter 2007/2008.

2. Multicoloured strips of satin and suede make up the silhouette of this geometric, block-heeled sandal. Winter 2010/2011.

3. Curved strips of suede in dusty pink, brown and black are highlighted with metallic gold piping on this wedge sandal. Winter 2011/2012.

Marc Jacobs

A simple kitten-heeled Mary Jane, with low-cut vamp in black kid leather. Spring/summer 2013.

Marc Jacobs was born in New York City in 1963. His huge success across all areas of fashion can be tracked back to his early years, when, after graduating from the High School of Art and Design in 1981 he entered Parsons School of Design. His time at Parsons saw him earn some of the school's highest honours, including Design Student of the Year for his graduate collection of oversized Op Art sweaters. The collection immediately thrust him into the limelight and almost overnight he was offered his own label.

In 1989 he and business partner Robert Duffy joined Perry Ellis as vice-president and president, respectively, of women's design. In 1992 they were honoured with the CFDA's Women's Designer of the Year award for the infamous 'Grunge' collection, a collection that lost them their tenure at the sportswear label, but which still has a huge influence on fashion some 20 years later.

In 1993 Jacobs went on to launch Marc Jacobs International alongside Robert Duffy. This is when he truly came into his own, bringing us joyous quirky creations, such as the inverted-heel shoe from his spring/summer 2008 collection, that are instantly recognizable. His innate ability to be on-trend and his constant pushing of the boundaries are paramount to Jacobs's success.

A fashion designer in the truest sense, the Jacobs empire spans every genre of design. From women's, men's and childrenswear to footwear and accessories, season upon season, Jacobs delivers collections that are as different as they are signature. Many of his designs draw on the 1960s and 1970s, but are given a modern Jacobs twist. Each of his labels, which include the Marc Jacobs main line and Marc by Marc Jacobs diffusion line, complements the other, creating a 360-degree vision of the designer's ethos.

His eclectic footwear collections are brought up to date with bold and unusual colour combinations and over-the-top silhouettes. For example, block heel 1960s-style pumps are shown in their original mustard yellow but with exaggerated hardware. His spring/summer 2013 resort collection saw Mary Janes modernized with a rounded heel in monochrome stripes and an elongated pointed toe. His women's shoe collections break the mould of conventional footwear design with traditional silhouettes and constructions eschewed for a twisted, almost surreal take on design. His ballerina-style 'Mouse' pumps are adorned with miniature ears, a nose and whiskers to resemble a cartoon mouse. This style has become a favourite among the fashion elite.

Wearing a Marc Jacobs shoe is all about making a statement. As with his clothes, there is a continuous undercurrent of caricature that makes them as crazy as they are wearable. Heels are literally inverted to create a construction that is seemingly impossible to wear, and buckles and trims are pumped up and supersized to cartoon-like proportions. Jacobs's success lies in his ability to tap into the zeitgeist of popular culture while still retaining a unique signature style. Copied by many, his work continues to appeal and inspire, and his empire continues to expand rapidly today.

1.

2.

5.

3.

1. A deep-red ankle boot with a square toe and Edwardian-style buckle feature on the vamp. The boot is modernized with a high block heel and cowboy-esque cut-out detailing on the quarters, revealing contrast colour. Fall/winter 2012.

2. The cowboy-detail style in powder blue.

3. A vibrant pink ankle boot with a square toe and Edwardian-style buckle in oversized diamanté. Fall/winter 2012.

4. A high, block-heeled square-toe shoe featuring three metal buckles and over-extended tongue detail. Fall/winter 2012.

5. The diamanté-buckle style in mustard yellow.

4.

1.

2.

5.

3.

4.

1. A metallic cobalt-blue shoe with an extreme square toe and a buckle in oversized diamanté featured on the vamp. Fall/winter 2012.

2. The black-leather version of the square-toe buckle shoe.

3. White clog-style sandal with circular diamanté closure and contrasting black platform sole. Fall/winter 2012.

4. A metallic silver leather mid-length boot with rounded square toe and diamanté buckles. Fall/winter 2012.

5. Oversized diamanté buckles feature on this chunky strappy platform sandal with marble-effect footbed. Fall/winter 2012.

1.

2.

1. A childlike colour-block
   loafer in contrasting neon
   yellow and hyper-bright red
   with a chunky white and
   electric-blue cleated sole.
   Resort 2013.

2. A chunky platform sandal
   with geometric printed
   wide straps in a 1970s-style
   pink and brown colour
   combination. Resort 2013.

3. Colour-block loafer in
   contrasting red and neon
   pink with a chunky white
   and navy blue cleated sole.
   Resort 2013.

3.

1.

1. A 1970s-style towering
platform with patent
leather straps, featuring
giant jewels and circular
diamanté buckle closure
on the straps. Resort 2013.

Nicholas Kirkwood

Styles from the spring/summer 2013 collection look book.

One of the most sought-after design talents in the footwear industry today, Nicholas Kirkwood has an unsurpassed ability to invent stunning architectural creations season after season. Kirkwood is a pioneer in driving a new attitude towards fresh, modern design and innovation, and there is no denying a shoe from him is a work of art.

Kirkwood studied at the world-renowned Central Saint Martins and Cordwainers College in London and worked for five years with milliner extraordinaire Philip Treacy before embarking on his own career. He launched his eponymous label in 2005 aged just 25, and his debut collection of architecturally inspired styles was deemed a triumph by the likes of style mavens Grace Jones, Daphne Guinness and the late Isabella Blow, as well as receiving rave reviews from industry insiders.

Kirkwood's aesthetic combines graphic silhouettes with beautiful bold lines; immediately striking, his shoes are sharp and considered. Choosing not to over-decorate, Kirkwood stays clear of superfluous detailing, instead using extreme colour combinations, exotic skins and unusual materials. His shoes are all handcrafted in Italy, using innovative techniques to develop custom-made materials such as degradé fabrics, python, rubberized leather and sueded alligator.

It goes without saying that those lucky enough to wear his shoes include a prize list of celebrities including Sarah Jessica Parker, Gwyneth Paltrow, Alexa Chung, Victoria Beckham and Florence Welch. Beyond his own label, Kirkwood has also worked with both established brands and emerging talent to create shoes for their runway shows – brands such as Fendi, Erdem and Peter Pilotto have been fortunate enough to work with this master of footwear.

In 2011 Kirkwood worked in collaboration with the Keith Haring Foundation to commemorate 20 years since the artist's death. Kirkwood's ten-piece collection of one-off designs includes some of Haring's less well-known artworks and brilliantly transforms 2D artwork into 3D wearable art. Known for pushing the limits of what can be walked in, this collection, including Swarovski-encrusted roller-skate boots, is no exception. Three styles using Haring's Tokyo graphics were also designed for the commercial market.

Since its launch in 2005, the Nicholas Kirkwood brand has continued to impress, awarded the Condé Nast/*Footwear News* Vivian Infantino award in 2005 for emerging talent and two years later the prestigious *Vogue Italia* Who is on Next award for accessory design. In 2011, Kirkwood won Condé Nast/*Footwear News* Designer of the Year, having previously won in 2008, and in 2012 earned both *Elle*'s Accessories Designer of the Year and the British Fashion Awards Accessories award, for the second time.

Opening his first flagship store on London's Mount Street in 2011, a year later Kirkwood opened his New York store, suitably based in the city's Meatpacking District. Kirkwood's success continues – in 2013 he received the prestigious British Fashion Council/*Vogue* Fashion Fund and in the same year launched his first standalone men's collection.

1. This black suede ankle
boot's delicate floral
embroidery is contrasted
with a super-engineered heel.
Fall/winter 2013.

2. A classic pointed stiletto
pump is given a new lease of
life with a super-engineered
heel in red. Fall/winter 2013.

3. Dramatic strappy evening
sandal with flower appliqué
and wire wrap ankle strap
covered with gold flat-link
chain. Fall/winter 2013.

4. Classic pointed stiletto
pump in contrast matt and
shine chevron stripes, with
shocking pink patent leather
heel. Fall/winter 2013.

1. Coloured python skin, ghillie laced boot with scalloped cut-out side panels, front fur panel and back zip closure. Fall/winter 2013.

2. Showstopping heel-less platform bootie, in monochrome marble-effect leather with back zip closure. Fall/winter 2013.

3. Round-toe pump with contrast coloured forepart platform and statement signature frill heel in candy-striped satin. Fall/winter 2013.

4. Peep-toe bootie with cut-out quarters, contrast fox-fur trim, metal cigarette heel and back zip closure. Fall/winter 2013.

1.

4.

2.

1. Towering multicoloured
   Mary Jane sandal with
   python heel, patent leather
   forepart platform and
   padded ankle strap in
   suede. Pre-fall 2013.

2. Sheer red lace statement
   pump with round toe, 13cm
   (5⅛in) hammered metal heel
   and forepart platform.
   Pre-fall 2013.

3. Caged T-bar sandal in
   scarlet suede and neon pink
   piping, with turquoise snake
   heel and forepart platform.
   Pre-fall 2013.

4. Green and turquoise scalloped
   and laced sandal with delicate
   stone embellishment and
   metal cigarette heel. Spring/
   summer 2013.

3.

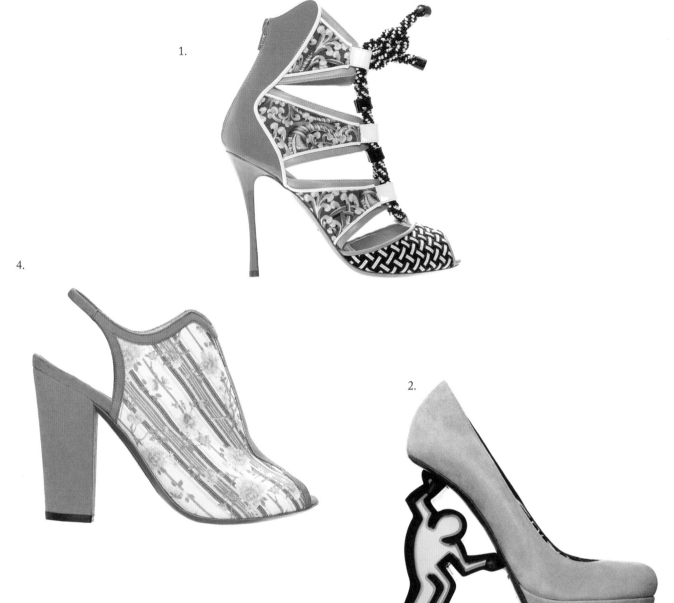

1.

4.

2.

3.

1. Peep-toe, ghillie lace-up sandal with floral print, woven and patent leather upper. Nicholas Kirkwood for Peter Pilotto runway show, spring/summer 2013.

2. Turquoise platform pump with iconic Keith Haring figure heel. Nicholas Kirkwood and Keith Haring Foundation collaboration 2011.

3. Printed T-bar platform sandal with notched pink metallic heel. Nicholas Kirkwood for Erdem, spring/summer 2013.

4. High-cut slingback sandal with floral print upper and poppy-red block heel and binding. Nicholas Kirkwood for Suno runway show, spring/summer 2013.

Zoe Lee

Gray (top), *Luling* (centre) and
Breau Bridge (below) from the
Zoe Lee spring/summer 2013
collection look book.

British-based designer Zoe Lee was born in
Toronto, Canada to a Japanese mother and
Canadian father. A graduate of Central Saint
Martins and the Royal College of Art, London,
Lee was tutored by the great master of footwear
himself, Manolo Blahnik, before launching her
own line of luxury footwear in January 2012.

What inspired you to get into footwear design?
The craft involved in making shoes and the hands-
on familiarity needed to work with such a variety
of materials is probably what drew me to footwear.
I've always been interested in this, and in the idea
of working on a three-dimensional object. That's
one side of design – the other is instinct and feeling,
which is the fashion aspect; the balancing of these
ideas is very enjoyable for me.

Do you have a particular kind of woman in mind when you are designing?
Not really. Your mood can decide what shoes you
choose to wear or buy. I think this informs me more
than having the characteristics of a particular person
in mind.

Where do you draw your inspiration from?
Colours that stick in my mind, places I go to, people
I meet – and the leather trade fair that I go to twice
a year. Often the most attractive things are beautiful
because of their context as well as their visual appeal.

Would you say you had a signature style? Describe it to us in five words.
Contradicting textures and storytelling colours.

When it comes to technique and fabric, are there particular styles and materials that run through each collection?
I am very interested in different textures and the
combining of these textures within a shoe or a
collection of shoes. I don't have defined themes
every season. I prefer to use the silhouette or style
of a shoe as the solid framework through which
interesting materials can be displayed. I suppose for
this reason I do often reuse silhouettes from season
to season, but I always try to change their context.

How do you see the current fascination with footwear developing?
It's strange how although a shoe is pretty much the
same shape on or off the foot, once it's on and it's
right, your foot (or you) are what's made it right.
The reason for the recent spotlight on footwear is
perhaps because the number of designers out there
has increased. There could be a saturation soon and
perhaps people will become more restrained and try
to edit more. That wouldn't be such a bad thing.

What are your ambitions for your brand in the future?
To grow consistently as a brand and at a pace that is
appropriate to the product. Also to enjoy all the good
and bad aspects of the industry and work with it.

1.

2.

3.

1. *Mamou* Flat closed-toe
   sandal with criss-cross strap
   detailing in iridescent silver,
   nude and cobalt-blue full-
   grain leather. Spring/
   summer 2013.

2. *Grand Chenier* Delicate caged
   sandal with criss-cross ankle
   strap in complementary tones
   of nude and grey leather.
   Spring/summer 2013.

3. *Iota* Platform pump with
   softly rounded toe, 11cm
   (4⅜in) tapered heel and fine
   ankle strap closure. Spring/
   summer 2013.

1. *Iota* Platform pump with
   softly rounded toe in metallic
   leather with 11cm (4⅜in)
   tapered heel and fine ankle
   strap closure. Spring/
   summer 2013.

2. *Gray* Heavy fronted sandal
   in fine basketweave leather
   with fine ankle strap and 7cm
   (2¾in) stacked Cuban heel.
   Spring/summer 2013.

3. *Luling* Perforated mock lace-
   up ankle boot with tie-dyed
   silk fabric ties and low heel.
   Spring/summer 2013.

1.

2.

3.

1.

2.

3.

1. *Meraux* Blue knotted T-bar
   pump, with fine ankle strap
   and 10.5cm (4in) heel, in
   crackled-effect leather.
   Spring/summer 2013.

2. *Breau Bridge* Closed-toe
   sandal with decorative ankle
   tie and 10.5cm (4in) heel,
   in moiré silk fabric. Spring/
   summer 2013.

3. *Vivian* Classic pump with
   tie-dyed chiffon ankle wrap
   detailing and 10.5cm (4in)
   heel, in cross-hatched white
   leather. Spring/summer 2013.

1.

2.

3.

1. *Theriot* Patchworked leather
   D'Orsay mid-height shoe,
   with knotted leather ankle
   tie closure and Cuban heel.
   Spring/summer 2013.

2. *Violet* Low-rise ankle boot
   with cross-ankle strap closure
   and 7cm (2¾in) block heel.
   Spring/summer 2013.

3. *Belle Rose* High-cut elasticated
   pump with softly pointed toe
   and 7cm (2¾in) Cuban heel.
   Spring/summer 2013.

Kat Maconie

Natasha Cobalt-blue cut-out bootie with peep-toe detailing and concealed platform. The ankle straps add a hard edge to the style. Fall/winter 2013.

Fusing her expertise in fashion design and buying with her keen attention to detail, designer Kat Maconie has been challenging the way we look at footwear since the launch of her label in 2009. Describing her shoes as 'wearable, lasting, understated, contemporary glamour,' the designer draws her inspiration from the city where she was born and raised – London. Maconie's understanding of what women love to wear can be traced to her fashion background. She trained at Tomasz Starzewski, Whistles and Sitting Pretty before taking a footwear design course at the London College of Fashion and launching her own footwear collection.

The city's often hectic lifestyle, which she summarizes as 'work / play / work / play!' is something Maconie bears in mind when designing for her customers. This train of thought and application is easy to see in her bold block heels that don't compromise on style and elegance, but nonetheless are essentially wearable day to day. The secret to the wearability of a Kat Maconie high heel can be found hidden in the sole. Fashion brands often favour thin leather soles, which look elegant but can be uncomfortable to wear. Maconie has developed a concealed insole that moulds to the wearer's foot, making the shoe more comfortable throughout the day.

The strong graphic lines and seemingly simple silhouettes that are fast becoming her signature style are reflective of the kind of woman she has in mind when designing. 'I have many muses… mostly my friends in London. The designs always get tested on them in my mind before being made into an actual sample: will they love them? If so they go in!' says Maconie.

Her stark colour-block designs are often adorned with metal hardware trims inspired by the vintage trinkets and jewellery she has discovered at London antique market Alfies and also Old Spitalfields Market. Metalwork is key to every Kat Maconie collection. Gold metal hardware, angular block heels and cut-out details have become key characteristics of her designs. The signature gold screw is a feature of every pair of Maconie shoes. 'I love detail, which is so important in shoe design – the tiniest detail can transform a shoe,' the designer elaborates.

When asked how she imagines women's fascination with footwear developing Maconie answers, 'New techniques and developments in footwear mean that shoes will continue to get more incredible and amazing, allowing shoe designers to be more ambitious and creative with their designs.'

Maconie's future plans include growing her international business and e-commerce site with hopes to have a standalone store in London soon. She is also looking to expand the range by launching a trainer line as well as a bag line, further accommodating the fast-living city women she designs for. 'I think a great pair of shoes can really change the way a woman feels – they can add confidence far more than any piece of clothing.'

1.

2.

3.

1. *Valerie* A matt-black pump
   silhouette with Cubist
   platform heel feature in violet
   and gold metal. Fall 2012.

2. *Velma* Sketch, in tomato-red
   suede. The peep-toe boot
   features a Cubist platform
   heel in black and gold metal.
   Fall 2012.

3. *Penny* Original sketch of this
   style (see next page).

1.

2.

4.

1. *Penny* A high-heeled loafer
   in metallic violet leather with
   block heel and concealed
   platform, featuring a
   suede bow adornment in
   contrasting black. Fall 2012.

2. *Cecelia* Red suede ballerina
   pump with metal studding on
   a bed of black suede on the
   back. Features rounded heel.
   Fall 2012.

3. *Ida* A black suede retro pump
   with concealed platform sole
   and contrast violet metallic
   ankle strap featuring a bow
   adornment in black suede.
   Fall 2012.

4. *Velma* Black leather peep-toe
   boot with a Cubist platform
   heel in black and gold metal.
   Fall 2012.

3.

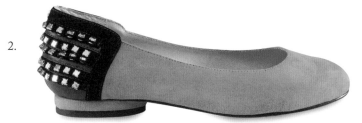

Marni

Tan leather sandal with pointed last, worn with the women's ready-to-wear collection for spring/summer 2013, Milan Fashion Week runway show.

Marni shoes are eclectic with a subtle retro feel, and instantly recognizable for their distinct use of colour and graphic prints. Solid block heels, wide straps and 1960s-inspired geometric prints are some of the elements central to Marni's designs. Functional silhouettes in raw-edge leather meet highly decorative semi-precious stones and beading, while chunky wooden-heeled sandals are a playful take on traditional sports sandals. From colour-blocked wedges and gladiator sandals to masculine lace-ups and heavy boots, Marni redefines luxury with its sophisticated utilitarian style.

Launched in 1994, the iconic label was founded by husband and wife team Consuelo and Gianni Castiglioni. Fascinated by fashion from an early age Consuelo, designer and creative director at Marni, began her career as a fashion consultant in Milan, where she met her husband Gianni. The Marni brand was established when the pair designed a collection for Gianni's father, the founder of Ciwifurs, one of Italy's largest leather and fur companies. Their collection redefined the perception of fur and how it could be used as a fabric; well received by press and stockists, it quickly developed into a complete collection of ready-to-wear apparel and accessories.

Marni continues to push the boundaries of modern design with each new collection and places huge emphasis on the product research and development side of its business. Today Marni has over 100 stores across the globe selling both women's and men's ready-to-wear and resort ranges, an accessory line and eyewear as well as shoes.

What inspired you to get into footwear design?
The footwear is related to the ready-to-wear collections. It was a natural process. I am a perfectionist and define every detail.

Do you have a particular kind of woman in mind when you are designing?
The woman who chooses Marni has an unconstrained way of expressing herself. I think she has a sophisticated approach to fashion, not necessarily too fashion-driven, but with a strong identity in terms of style. She is curious and enthusiastic about experimenting and playing with forms, structures, prints and colours, and creating her own combinations.

Where do you draw your inspiration from?
Inspiration can come from anything that is around me – it can be art, photography, a scrap of wallpaper, a country or a book. Life itself is inspiring.

Would you say you had a signature style? Describe it to us in five words.
Modern, comfortable, versatile, unique, eclectic.

When it comes to technique and fabric, are there particular styles and materials that run through each collection?
I love playing with contradictory elements, combining for example couture and technical materials. The contradictions give an unexpected touch to my collections, something that takes time to discover.

How do you see the current fascination with footwear developing?
Accessories have always been very important to me. They 'frame' the look.

What are your ambitions for your brand in the future?
To continue with new and exciting projects and challenges.

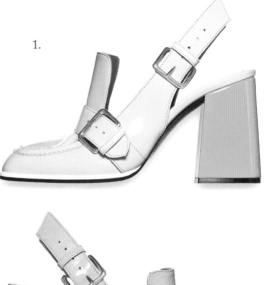

1.

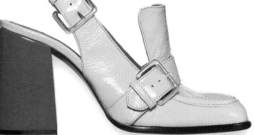

3.

2.

1. Patent leather pump with
   flared heel and buckle
   detailing, in white and
   yellow and peach and
   herb variations. Summer
   edition 2013.

2. Patent leather platform
   loafer with raw-edge calfskin
   apron and leather strap with
   metal press-stud detailing.
   Resort 2013.

3. Closed-toe platform sandal
   with red patent leather heel,
   velvet upper and platform
   and gold toe and ankle strap.
   Fall/winter 2012/2013.

1.

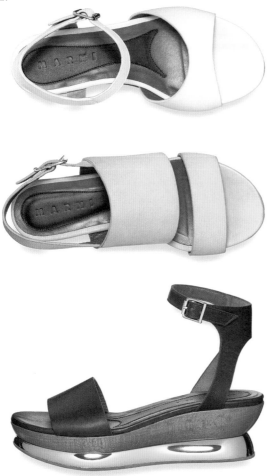

2.

1. Platform sandal with raw-
   edge leather straps and a
   wooden platform with the
   lower section galvanized in
   pure gold, featuring various
   uppers. Spring/summer 2013.

2. Hourglass-shaped wedge
   sandal with crossed straps in
   raw-edge calfskin, pointed
   last and wood and metal
   covered heel. Resort 2013.

1.

3.

2.

1. Three variations of a Fussbett
   sandal in black suede with
   jewel-encrusted straps
   featuring faceted crystals
   and metal spike studs.
   Resort 2013.

2. Flat Mary Jane with cleated
   sole, wide buckled ankle strap
   and gold contrast toe. Also
   shown, variation without toe
   cap. Winter 2012.

3. Two-tone kiltie fringed
   golfing shoe with cleated
   sole and lace tie closure.
   Winter 2012.

1.

2.

3.

1. Woven platform sandal in black and white suede with ribbed heel and decorative gold-ribbed platform. Fall/winter 2012/2013.

2. Suede T-bar platform sandal and wedge sandal, both with decorative toe strap in grosgrain ribbon encrusted with cut crystals and gold spiked studs. Resort 2013.

3. Block-heel sandal with crossed straps in raw-edge calfskin, and wood and leather block heel. Spring/summer 2013.

Marsèll

Transcending fashion trends with their own inimitable style, Milan-based Italian footwear brand Marsèll specializes in handcrafted shoes with a distinctly worn-in patina. Softly structured silhouettes, turned-up toes and raw-edge leather detailing are just some of the qualities central to its utilitarian design aesthetic. Created in 2001, the brand manufactures its shoes in Italy, in-house, in small quantities and with meticulous attention to detail.

What inspired you to get into footwear design?
We got into footwear design because shoes are challenging design objects, and we like challenges. We are all individuals but what we share is a passion for artisan craft and a desire to create something innovative. Marsèll is the outcome of this shared passion: a mingling of streamlined design, high-end craft and out-of-the-box communication.

On a larger scale, we have always conceived of style as more than just the creation of pieces of clothing or footwear. This led to the creation in 2009 of the Marsèlleria Permanent Exhibition, our multidisciplinary incubator for shows, happenings and performances in Milan. It gives new energy to our creative process and inspiration.

Do you have a particular kind of woman in mind when you are designing?
Our creative process is focused on the object, not on the marketing of the audience. That said, we think Marsèll speaks to anyone who likes innovative design mixed with excellence in craft.

Where do you draw your inspiration from?
Our creative process is wholly design-driven. We start from sturdy, classic shapes; a detail is then overblown to give it visual prominence, or is totally erased; a slice or a hole can turn into design statements.

Would you say you had a signature style? Describe it to us in five words.
A Marsèll shoe is understated, yet the signature style is quite evident. We'd describe it as subtle, muted, solid, visionary and utilitarian.

When it comes to technique and fabric, are there particular styles and materials that run through each collection?
Marsèll expresses a solid yet tactile take on shoe design. Materials, for this reason, are pivotal. Signature details that run through the collections are traditional finishes used to give a lived-in, contemporary patina to our models, soles and heels. Extra-long shoelaces, or a lack of them whatsoever, recur as well.

How do you see the current fascination with footwear developing?
'God is in the details', so Mies van der Rohe used to say. Stating that shoes can make or break a look is almost a pleonasm. Over the last few years as clothes design has focused heavily on vintage sources, so creativity has focused more and more on shoes and accessories. Shoes deal with an irrational side of the human psyche, which actually adds a layer of mystery and magic to what we do.

What are your ambitions for your brand in the future?
To still employ the level of craft and invention that has led us to this point, and to do so while exploring the most exciting areas of contemporary visual culture.

1.

2.

5.

3.

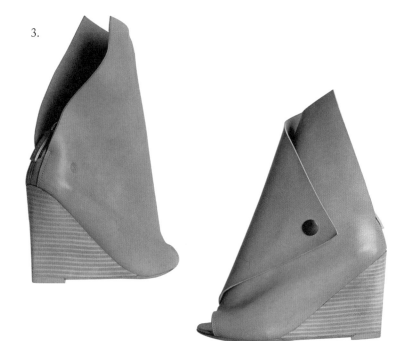

1. *Trivellina* Soft peep-toe lace-up ankle boot with sculpted leather stacked heel and punched leather eyelets. Spring/summer 2012.

2. *Pennola* Raw-edge, chunky T-bar sandal with solid stacked leather heel and red leather quarter. Spring/summer 2013.

3. *Muro* Architectural grey leather ankle boot with wedge heel and fold-over-and-press stud closure. Spring/summer 2013.

4. *Nola* Taupe suede ankle boot featuring unique toe-to-heel lacing detail and leather laces with stacked leather wedge heel. Fall/winter 2011/2012.

5. *Pennola* Peep-toe ankle bootie with high-cut quarters, front panel insert, and stacked leather heel. Spring/summer 2011.

4.

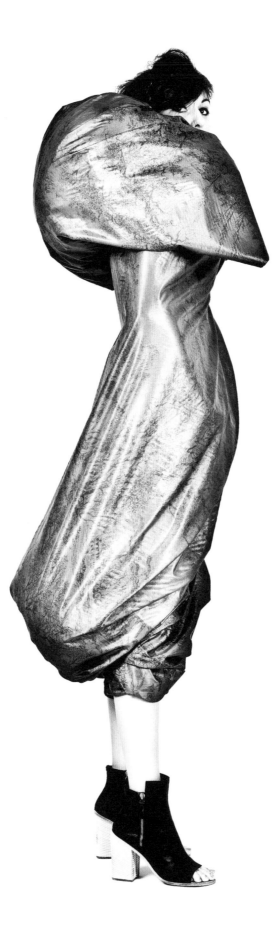

1. 2010 Marsèll advertising
campaign, ruched leather
ankle boot modelled by
Valentina Suma, styled by
artist Agne Raceviciute and
photographed by Mirko Rizzi.

Daniele Michetti

Dominic Slashed and woven leather ankle boot with hidden forepart platform, featured here in red and black. Fall/winter 2013/2014.

Established in 2009, the Italian brand Daniele Michetti can best be described as cutting-edge luxury. Michetti's eclectic and untiring style ranges from extreme deconstruction to haute fashion and refined elegance. He is a designer who is constantly driving forward new developments in materials, colours and textures.

Handcrafted techniques play a major role in the designer's collections. His signature shoe, an open-toe stiletto with wrapped woven leather bands, is a great example of the level of skill and quality of craftsmanship that goes into creating these works of art. Choosing to keep his silhouettes clean, Michetti's greatest ability lies in balancing avant-garde detailing with perfect proportions.

Particularly fond of materials with movement and transparency, Michetti likes to use leathers with a natural finish, such as calf, kid and patent, as well as more exotic leathers such as python, crocodile and stingray. Not afraid to use colour in his collections, Michetti loves to work with suede for its ability to hold a real depth of tone.

While highly cutting edge, Daniele Michetti shoes have a timeless quality, which is due in part to the designer's source of inspiration. Rather than researching a particular era or style, Michetti tends to be inspired by the moment. 'There are places that have become almost customary to visit when travelling for business or pleasure: museums, exhibitions, markets, cities. I find the most curious inspirations when I happen to find myself in situations by chance, and quite often they become my starting point for a new creation,' he explains.

Born in Corridonia, Italy in September 1976 into the family shoe business, Michetti was still very young when he took his first steps into the world of footwear, attending various specialist courses. His first real experience came when he worked at Italian brand Santoni (1995–2005) as designer and product manager. It was an experience that fuelled his passion for luxury, beauty and innovation, three elements that are clearly evident in his own collections today. Michetti's flair and professional excellence were instrumental in Santoni's success, helping to develop and refine the family-run business into an established name in men's footwear.

International recognition came in 2009 when Michetti took first prize in the accessories category at the Who is on Next competition organized by *Vogue Italia* and Altaroma. This prestigious award spurred the designer on to market his new collection, which was immediately picked up by some of the world's best-known stores.

On his road to success, Daniele Michetti has always paid particular attention to his clients' needs. He is constantly developing his footwear knowledge by perfecting the quality of his product, employing technical professionals and specialized workshops, and refining his detail and construction techniques.

Michetti's constant drive and dedication has already seen him work with the likes of Burberry Prorsum and Yves Saint Laurent, and he is currently working with direct product responsibility for influential Italian footwear companies Sergio Rossi and Tod's.

1.

2.

4

1. *Deidre* Stiletto zip-up
   ankle boot in petrol blue
   and black contrasting size
   houndstooth leather. Fall/
   winter 2013/2014.

2. *Dolores* Graphic stiletto
   bootie in contrasting size
   woven houndstooth and
   black leather, with dipped
   top-line and back zip closure.
   Fall/winter 2013/2014.

3. *Anita* Signature style with
   satin-wrapped woven bands,
   beaded straps, decorative
   back zip closure and stiletto
   heel. Spring/summer 2013.

4. *Becka* Printed python-
   skin pump with signature
   studded draped heel cape and
   cigarette heel. Fall/winter
   2013/2014.

3.

1.

4.

2.

3.

1. A selection of styles including the *Dolores* from the fall/winter 2013 collection.

2. *Cora* Woven chevron T-bar sandal featuring an extended double ankle cuff with pinked edging and metal eyelet detailing. Spring/summer 2013.

3. *Carina* Laced peep-toe bootie in black and peach woven chevron with back zip closure. Spring/summer 2013.

4. *Cleo* Monochrome black and white caged sandal with decorative metal eyelets and pinked strap edging. Spring/summer 2013.

1.

2.

4.

3.

1. *Diocle* Flat suede slipper with contrasting red python block heel and black looped decorative detailing. Fall/winter 2013/2014.

2. *Clover* Highly decorative flat sandal with fringing, graphic monochrome black and white panels and tiny decorative eyelets. Spring/summer 2013.

3. *Coline* Nude leather strappy sandal with spiked metal stud detailing and signature draped leather heel cape. Spring/summer 2013.

4. *Daisy* Stiletto bootie with hidden forepart platform, and inserts of black and white oversized woven leather and suede. Fall/winter 2013/2014.

1.

3.

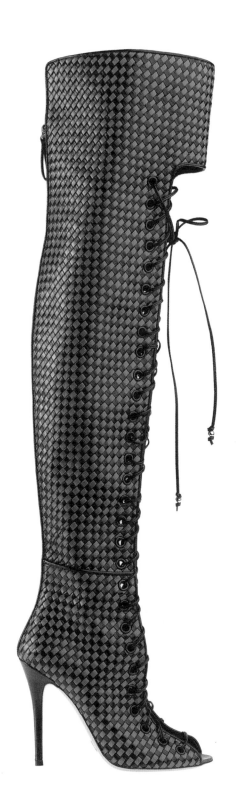

2.

1. *Becka* A classic nude leather
pump with signature studded
draped leather heel cape and
cigarette heel in gold. Spring/
summer 2013.

2. *Deva* Sexy over-the-knee
peep-toe boot in green and
black woven houndstooth
with toe-to-knee lacing. Fall/
winter 2013/2014.

3. *Diletta* Minimal stiletto
sandal in purple suede
featuring red python heel and
ankle strap and black patent
bow. Fall/winter 2013/2014.

Chie Mihara

Gefren (spring/summer 2012), *Teco* (spring/summer 2010) and *Kristi* (spring/summer 2012) photographed at the designer's studio in Spain.

Chie Mihara's shoes carry a wonderfully nostalgic charm that is difficult to pin down to any one era, elevating them above design clichés to become instantly desirable. Her shoes combine a unique blend of comfort and style and are immediately recognizable for their signature rounded last and handcrafted aesthetic.

Born in Brazil to Japanese parents, Mihara lived in Fukuoka, Japan for five years from the age of 18, studying fashion design at the Kyushu Designer Gakuin and working for Junko Koshino as a design assistant. She later moved to New York to study Accessory Design at the Fashion Institute of Technology before working for accessory designer Sam & Libby in New York. Mihara finally settled in Spain in 1995 where she worked for renowned French footwear designer Charles Jourdan before launching her own label.

Comfort has played a pivotal role in the Chie Mihara philosophy from the very beginning. Established in 2002, the brand was launched to offer women something different – footwear designed by women for women. With this in mind, comfort and style are placed at the very heart of her designs, so much so that every shoe features an anatomical footbed designed specifically to accommodate a woman's foot. 'I want my shoes to be beautiful, and beauty must also be comfortable,' she explains.

Colour plays a key role in Mihara's design process. Indeed colour is the starting point for each new collection, with every season seeing Mihara go to great lengths to develop her own unique leather dyes. It is the combination of these bespoke colour palettes and patina leathers that lend her shoes their distinct character and familiar charm.

Mihara's shoes display many of the techniques and constructions employed by a traditional master craftsman. True to her artisan's approach, Mihara works exclusively with leather, creating her own shoe ornamentation out of leather and by hand. By working directly with the leathers she is able to develop and explore endless design possibilities. 'You'll be amazed by how many ideas flow from four straps of leather!' she says.

Drawing inspiration from a number of sources, Mihara is particularly influenced by the 1930s, 1960s and 1980s and her hand-sculpted lasts, rounded toe shapes and heavy profiled heels are indicative of these eras. Referencing vintage details, she skilfully reworks them in leather with her own unique blend of plaiting, pleating and ruching.

Mihara's multicultural background has had a significant role in creating her unique design style. Brazil has informed her feminine detailing, Japan her approach to design, the US her practicality and Spain, her home country, is the place where the foundations of her brand were built.

With over 1,000 clients worldwide including Neiman Marcus and Bergdorf Goodman in the US, Selfridges in the UK, Isetan in Japan and Le Bon Marché in Paris, Mihara's success is unprecedented. She now has her sights set firmly on the future with the possibility of developing a totally new line of androgynous footwear with an avant-garde feel.

1.

2.

1. *Zosh* Vintage-style brogue loafer in embossed crocodile, featuring a round toe, 8cm (3⅛in) stacked tapered heel and forepart platform. Fall/ winter 2012/2013.

2. *Uja Pepper* Vintage-style platform sandal in embossed crocodile with cut-out leaf detailing, stacked heel and forepart platform. Fall/winter 2012/2013.

1.

2.

1. *Vulcano* Modern retro
   patchwork sandal with
   punched leather and
   leaf appliqué detailing.
   Featured here in two colour
   combinations. Spring/
   summer 2012.

2. *Terelu* Caged chunky sandal
   in suede, metallic and plain
   leather combination, with
   stacked suede heel and
   covered forepart platform.
   Spring/summer 2011.

Miu Miu

A chunky Mary Jane on the runway, in a silver and black colour combination. The elegant toe shape is offset by the heavy sole and fluted heel. Fall 2013.

The story of the Miu Miu brand started back in 1992, when Miuccia Prada, the president of the Prada Group, decided that a younger sister was needed to expand the brand. Miu Miu has since become one of the leading high-fashion labels in the world. The division between the brands is instantly identifiable. While Prada looks to its heritage and classic chic, Miu Miu appeals to a younger, more trend-led woman.

'Avant-garde, sensual and provocative' are words that the brand uses to describe its essence, all of which can be seen in its footwear collections, season upon season. 'Miu Miu targets women driven by a modern spirit of exploration and experimentation in their fashion choices.'

Prada's association with, and dedication to, the arts filters down into its sister brand. Launched in 2012, 'Women's Tales' is a silent short-film series commissioned by Miuccia Prada for Miu Miu, in which high-profile female film directors explore stories about women, showcasing the brand's clothing. Directors include Zoe Cassavetes, Lucrecia Martel and Ava DuVernay.

Enterprises like this give Miu Miu a unique image and identity within the fashion arena. The brand's advertising is also a distinguishable feature that ensures the brand stands out from the competition. By using current avant-garde faces, the brand continually reinforces its slightly edgy appeal. Perennially cool and unconventional Chloë Sevigny was the face of Miu Miu in 1996 and again in 2012, while Kirsten Dunst, Maggie Gyllenhaal and Lindsay Lohan are just some of the other quirky names that have featured in their main campaigns.

All of these elements in combination are also visible in Miu Miu's footwear collections. Literally keeping the fashion cognoscenti on their toes, Miuccia Prada changes the pace every season. The fall/winter 2012 collection saw exaggerated silhouettes take on new proportions. Oversized platforms were teamed with Edwardian-style fluted heels and full uppers in luxurious materials. This juxtaposition of materials and references embodies the provocative Miu Miu spirit.

For spring/summer 2013, however, Miuccia did what she does best and presented a complete change. While still managing to retain the essence of the Miu Miu girl, the silhouettes were altogether more refined and ladylike in their proportions. The fluted heel was still there, but it had been whittled down into a more sophisticated and sexy stiletto; elsewhere, traces of coquettish allure could be found in a subversive pink pump, evoking a sexy secretary vibe.

As Miuccia Prada said of the collection, 'I was trying to be very elegant in a very different way… the femme fatale is never perfect… at least the ones I like.'

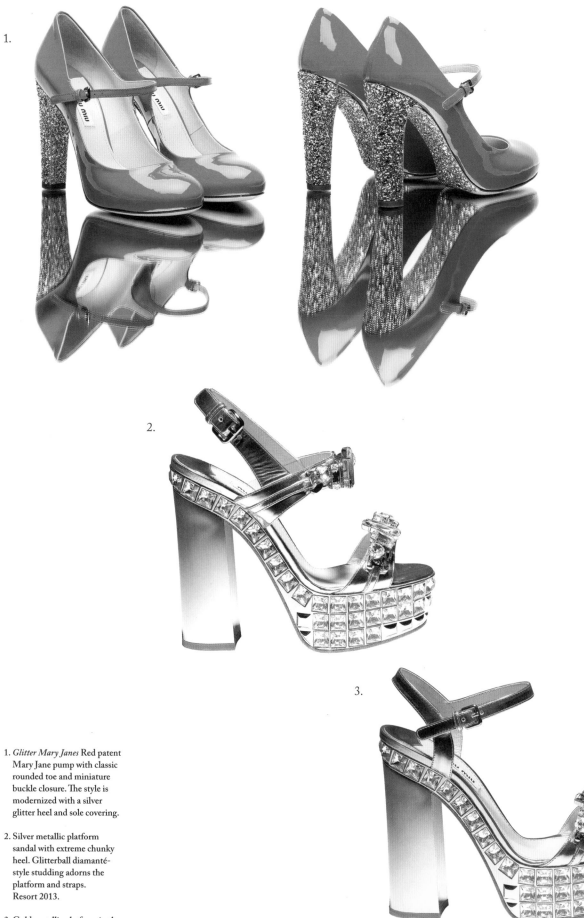

1.

2.

3.

1. *Glitter Mary Janes* Red patent Mary Jane pump with classic rounded toe and miniature buckle closure. The style is modernized with a silver glitter heel and sole covering.

2. Silver metallic platform sandal with extreme chunky heel. Glitterball diamanté-style studding adorns the platform and straps. Resort 2013.

3. Gold metallic platform in the same style. Resort 2013.

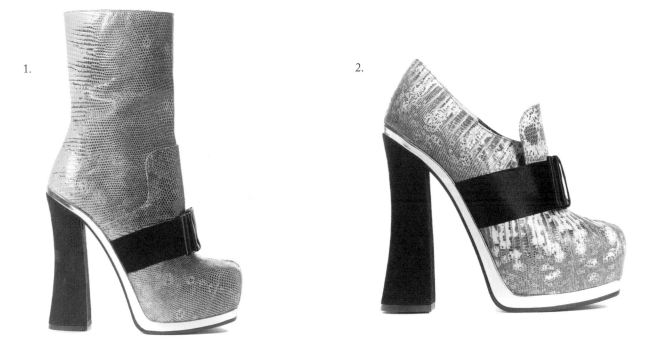

1. The ankle boot is transformed with a two-tone snakeskin upper and square toe silhouette. The deep wall of the toe shape is offset with a chunky fluted heel. Fall/winter 2012.

2. A heavy-set loafer with deep wall and stub toe silhouette in a monochrome snakeskin upper. The loafer tab and substantial fluted heel are covered in contrasting black leather. Fall/winter 2012.

3. Vivid green suede adds a contemporary edge to this retro platform sandal, with a silver metallic layer running through the sole. Resort 2013.

4. A simple flatform sandal style in red suede takes on an evening edge with glitterball diamanté-style studding on a chunky heel. Resort 2013.

1.

4.

2.

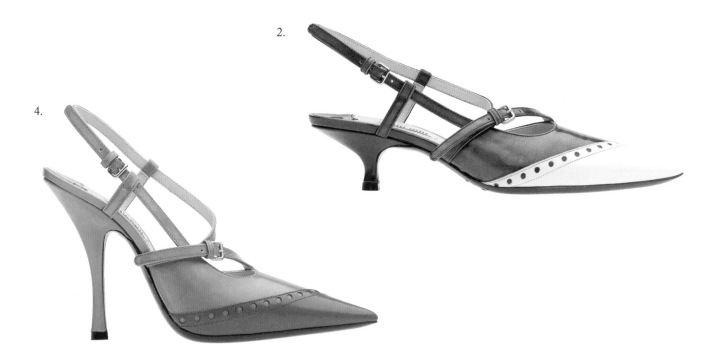

1. *Two-Toned* A flat slingback
   pump with pointed toe
   featuring two-tone brogue
   detailing. The double
   slingback adds a contemporary
   slant to the classic style.
   Spring/summer 2013.

2. *Two-Toned* A kitten-heel
   slingback with brogue
   detailing on a pointed
   toe and asymmetric strap
   detail on the vamp. Spring/
   summer 2013.

3. *Two-Toned* With brogue
   detailing on a pointed toe
   and asymmetric double
   slingback detail, this bronze
   and white style is from
   spring/summer 2013.

3.

4. *Two-Toned* A pointed
   slingback high heel in two-
   tone red and pink, with
   asymmetric strap detail
   on the vamp. Spring/
   summer 2013.

1.

2.

3.

1. A classic pointed pump with Louis heel in deep red satin. The 'bracelet' trim across the upper adds an evening touch. Spring/summer 2013.

2. *Craquelé* A classic pointed pump with Louis heel is brought up to date in a crackled powder-pink leather. Spring/summer 2013.

3. *Craquelé* The same style in dark olive green leather, setting off the gold leather underneath. Spring/summer 2013.

Chrissie Morris

Stephanie (above), black peep-toe bootie with stingray detailing, and *Saffi* (below), an ornate Deco sandal with laser-cut panel in exotic skin, both from fall/winter 2010. Photography by Kira Lillie.

Highly coveted, Chrissie Morris's feminine and flamboyant shoes are sold in prestigious stores and high-end boutiques around the world. With a distinctive style that combines British innovation with Italian craftsmanship, her shoes are instantly recognizable for their geometric detailing and daring use of colour, reminiscent of the Art Deco period.

Morris started designing at the age of 11. Having studied Fashion Design with a focus on knitwear and constructed textiles at Liverpool's John Moores University in the UK, she moved to Italy to complete her MA at Milan's Domus Academy. It was during this period, while finishing her master's degree in knitwear, that Morris started to experiment with leather and turned her focus to shoes. She was later hired as a footwear designer for the Spanish brand Sinela Gallery before launching her own label in 2007.

After debuting her first collection in the spring of 2008, Morris quickly achieved success. In the same year she won the accessories category in *Vogue Italia*'s prestigious Who is on Next award for emerging talent, and was awarded Best New Talent by US Condé Nast's *Footwear News*. It was a great start to a career that had only just set out in the world of footwear design.

One of the reasons why Morris has enjoyed swift success is her innate ability to understand the needs of her core customer. She knows what they require in terms of design and functionality, and focuses her priorities on comfort, quality and craftsmanship, all of which she does without question. 'I value what an active woman wants in a shoe; what she desires from

both a practical and poetic standpoint,' she explains. Although perhaps not for the fainthearted, her shoes are designed for strong independent women who, like Morris, appreciate beautiful design.

Morris's eclectic inspirations span a wide range of references from art history, fashion and architecture to science fiction. Her shoes are both innovative and highly sophisticated and have been described as 'Jewels for the feet'. She confidently mixes exotic skins such as lizard and python with wood and semi-precious stones and unexpected colour combinations. Her collections feature both graphic colour-blocking and more intricate decorative piping and appliqué.

The level of workmanship and minute attention to detail is indicative of the brand's philosophy. Morris's work ethic is firmly rooted in the true understanding of what it means to be 'Made in Italy'. Her shoes, entirely manufactured in the country, are also handmade under one roof. This style of manufacturing allows her complete autonomy and control of the production process from start to finish, resulting in shoes that truly embody the Italian artisan spirit.

As she continues to be inspired by Italy and its rich wealth of knowledge and traditional manufacturing techniques, what Morris hopes to accomplish in the long term – from both a personal and business perspective – is to help protect and preserve the dying art of traditional Italian footwear craftsmanship.

1.

2.

4.

3.

1. *Metropolis* Peep-toe pump
   with sleek piping and
   shimmering hits of stingray,
   with a notched heel cap and
   hidden platform. Spring/
   summer 2013.

2. *Farrah* Colour-blocked
   stingray sandal with nubuck
   ankle strap and heel. Light-
   reflective grey nylon is used
   for piping and sole. Spring/
   summer 2013.

3. *Ida* Colour-blocked clog in
   waxed stingray with yellow
   snake trim and nubuck block
   heel. Resort 2013.

4. *Clara* Sandal with glazed
   iridescent python upper,
   glass cabochon accessories,
   patent strap, nubuck heel and
   grey light-reflective nylon
   piping and sole. Spring/
   summer 2013.

1. *Bis* Nude leather multi-strap platform sandal with transparent mesh inserts, black piping, covered forepart platform and faceted heel. Resort 2013.

2. *Ann* Art Deco-inspired pointed stiletto pump in black suede with a fan of petal appliqué in lizardskin and silver piping. Fall/winter 2012/2013.

3. *Agatha* Art Deco-inspired suede sandal with petal appliqué in lizardskin and gold piping with stingray heel. Fall/winter 2012/2013.

4. *Alena* Black suede lace-up platform sandal with petal appliqué in lizardskin and gold piping, with tasselled laces. Fall/winter 2012/2013.

1.

2.

4.

3.

1. *Templies* Inspired by the
   Memphis Art Movement,
   this peep-toe pump has a
   fantastical sculptural heel
   with stingray appliqué and
   stud detailing. Fall/winter
   2012/2013.

2. *Rubiks* Suede peep-toe pump
   with hidden platform and
   cubes of brightly coloured
   squares in a criss-cross patent
   leather frame. Resort 2013.

3. *Magica* Simple flat sandal
   with multicoloured toe and
   ankle straps. Resort 2013.

4. *Nancy* Peep-toe T-bar
   platform sandal inspired by
   the Memphis Art Movement
   with Cubist heel and stingray
   and stud detailing. Fall/
   winter 2012/2013.

1.

2.

3.

1. *Ida* Inspired by Dr. Scholl
   sandals, blue stingray and
   suede slingback clog with
   wide-buckled straps and
   stacked leather block heel.
   Resort 2013.

2. *Clara* Slingback sandal in
   tones of glazed iridescent
   blue python and stingray,
   embellished with red
   oblong cabochons.
   Spring/summer 2013.

3. *Farrah* Inspired by jellies, a
   transparent python slingback
   sandal with black heel, ankle
   strap and piping and contrast
   orange buckle. Spring/
   summer 2013.

Charlotte Olympia

Look book imagery of the *Suede Priscilla in Stripes* platform pump with rounded toe and stiletto heel from the 'Over the Moon' fall/winter 2012/2013 collection.

'Women who like to dress from the feet up' is how British-based designer Charlotte Olympia Dellal describes her customers. Her bold colour palettes and love of animal prints hark back to Hollywood's golden age. Her 'island' platform, towering heels and trademark gold spiderweb motif are a contemporary take on the glamour of the 1940s and 50s.

Luxury footwear and accessories designer Dellal initially began designing out of a love for fashion and the art of corsetry. She developed her skills further at Cordwainers College for footwear and accessories design in London. Shortly after graduating Dellal launched her own London-based footwear label Charlotte Olympia in January 2008.

Since then the brand has made a significant impact on the world of footwear. The iconic 'Dolly' shoe with its signature metallic-gold 'island' platform and the cat-embroidered slipper 'Kitty' have become the brand's signature pieces and must-haves for the discerning woman's wardrobe. Celebrity advocates include fashion mavens Alexa Chung and Anna Dello Russo and stars Katy Perry and Beyoncé.

Instantly recognizable for features such as distinctive leopard prints, fan detailing and daring use of colour, the Charlotte Olympia shoe is both playful and sophisticated. Completely handmade in Italy and produced from the finest leathers and materials, an Olympia shoe is reputed for its exquisite detail and impeccable craftsmanship.

The shoes are designed around a specific narrative or theme, which is often skilfully depicted through whimsical embroidery or appliqué. Being part British, part Brazilian, a central source of inspiration for Dellal is South America. For spring/summer 2011 she headed home with a collection inspired by singer Carmen Miranda and her iconic fruit-laden hats, entitled 'Blame it on Rio'. Wooden block heels, vivid-coloured silks and leopard-print linen celebrated the samba and the carnival spirit of Brazilian culture.

The spring/summer 2012 'Sirens' collection was based on the glamour of Miami in the 1950s. Using the pastel colours famously associated with Miami's Art Deco architecture, her collection of heels and platforms featured deckchair stripes, flamingo feathers, pearls and seashells. Highlights of the collection included the banana-leaf platform sandal named 'Leaf me Alone'.

2012 also saw the brand launch a bridal collection. Under the fitting name 'Runaway Bride' it does for cream satin what Chanel did for tweed, namely gives it a modern makeover. With the Charlotte Olympia range of heels, wedges, platforms and flats 'Runaway Bride' is far removed from the classic wedding shoe collection and instead features materials such as leather, lace and leopard print.

Continually developing its line of footwear and accessories, the Charlotte Olympia brand is sold in some of the world's most prestigious stores and boutiques including Neiman Marcus and Bergdorf Goodman. Dellal currently creates four collections a year, as well as 'Runaway Bride', 'Encore' (a collection of signature styles available all year round), 'Cosmic' (a collection of Zodiac-inspired shoes and perspex clutch bags), 'Incy' (a collection of little shoes for little girls) and 'Tailor Made', a bespoke service.

1.

4.

2.

1. *Rapunzel* A towering plaited raffia wedge with decorative detailing and silk georgette wraparound ankle tie, from the 'Sirens' spring/summer 2012 collection.

2. *Serenade* Whimsical music-note wedge with moiré silk upper and delicate ankle strap with crystal buckle fastening. 'Over the Moon' collection. Fall/winter 2012.

3. *Coquette* Flirtatious and feminine, this playful satin boudoir mule is topped with a poodle head, trimmed in marabou feathers. 'La Vie En Rose' collection. Spring/summer 2013.

4. *Cherie* Fabulous pink sculptured poodle-heel sandal, bejewelled with crystal eyes and collar and heart-shaped charm. 'La Vie En Rose' collection. Spring/summer 2013.

3.

1.

4.

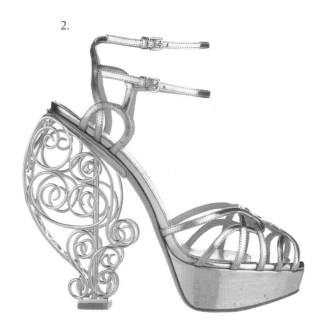

2.

3.

1. *Bruce* A statement silk sandal with covered platform, pleated upper, ankle strap and embellished gold leopard head charm. 'Encore' collection.

2. *Atlantis* A showstopping strappy gold leather sandal with double ankle strap fastening and beautifully sculpted ornate metal heel. 'Sirens' collection. Spring/ summer 2012.

3. *Dolly* Charlotte Olympia's most iconic shoe, with its distinctive metallic gold signature 'island' platform and covered heel. 'Encore' collection.

4. *Eve* This striking laced sandal bootie in soft laser-cut suede resembles lush tropical leaves. 'Encore' collection.

1.

2.

3.

1. *Bananas is my Business* A fruit-laden peep-toe sandal with solid wooden heel and wooden 'island' platform. 'Blame it on Rio' collection. Spring/summer 2011.

2. *Luna* Moon-face pump with satin upper and metallic leather crescent moon appliqué with embroidery and crystal teardrop detailing. 'Over the Moon' collection. Fall/winter 2012/2013.

3. *Bahia* Features a knotted toe strap and an intricate wooden inlaid heel and platform, depicting a tropical island scene. 'Glamazon' cruise 2013 collection.

1.

2.

1. *Botanica* Fantastical tropical
sandal with bamboo-covered
heel and platform. Patent
leather straps are adorned
with orchids. 'Glamazon'
cruise 2013 collection.

2. *Arlena in Excess* This highly
decorative T-bar sandal
features crystal-embellished
heel and straps and ornate
cameo charm. 'To Die For'
collection. Fall/winter
2011/2012.

Minna Parikka

Kide Fabulous glitter platform with purple metallic upper and cross-over buckle strap closure, from the fall/winter 2013/2014 look book.

'May these shoes lead you to new adventures.' So goes the mantra of Finnish accessory designer Minna Parikka, whose brand creates contemporary footwear that encompasses a world of fantasy, surrealism and playfulness.

Parikka's design motivation comes first and foremost from a love of shoes and fashion. She also places great emphasis on her ethos of having fun and being an individual in whatever you do and whatever you wear. 'I am lucky – I can be taken seriously as I negotiate business figures wearing bunny-ear shoes and then in the next moment I can put on my biker boots and go for a ride on my motorbike. It is important to express yourself and decide what you want to be – and not let others decide for you,' she says.

This spirit is carried through in a literal sense to her design work, where contrast and fantastical romanticism rule the roost. When designing, Parikka throws caution to the wind. Preferring to mix things up, she will happily juxtapose seemingly contradictory fabrics, textures and colours. Fluorescent embossed snakeskin is paired with grey leather, and wooden platform soles are matched with coloured acrylic heels.

These deliberate contrasts are central to the Minna Parikka design aesthetic. While best known for their playful signature detailing, Parikka's shoes also have a forceful side – her shoes are fun but are also designed to empower the wearer. So the light-hearted sentiment of bunny ears and love heart cut-outs (referencing 1950s-style pin-up girls) is paired with vertiginous heels and cutaway platforms to deliver bolder graphic statements.

As part of her creative process, Parikka likes to design with a specific character and narrative in mind. 'She's an independent woman who can be playful with her persona. She doesn't need to ask for anyone's permission and likes to make her own decisions,' she explains. Naturally, her shoes strike a chord with strong personalities; this is evident from her A-list devotees who include Lady Gaga, Beth Ditto and Paloma Faith, all of whom are very individual characters with a distinct sense of style.

Having discovered her footwear calling at the age of 15, Parikka moved to England four years later to pursue a degree in footwear design at De Montfort University, Leicester. She spent the next six years living, working and soaking up the unique qualities of Europe's most fashionable cities. In 2005 she returned to her native Helsinki to establish the Minna Parikka brand, launching her first footwear collection in 2006.

Since launching her brand, Parikka has steadily introduced new areas of interest such as bags and scarves and hopes to continue doing so in the future. 'I want to build a complete Minna Parikka universe around my shoes. I want to expand the collection to other accessories as well as men's shoes in the future. My dream is to have a whole shoe and accessory emporium.'

1. *Art* 1940s-style peep-toe
platform sandal with black
and white upper, lizard
appliqué, lemon-yellow
heel and forepart platform.
Spring/summer 2013.

2. *Ira* Mirror metallic winged
platform mule with peep
toe, tiered forepart platform,
chunky heel and pink heel
panel. Spring/summer 2013.

3. *Empire* Wooden platform
pump with pink acrylic heel
in black suede with ribbon
lacing. Spring/summer 2013.

4. *Deco* 1940s-style, colour-
blocked pastel peep-toe
platform sandal with
snake heel and folded
decorative appliqué.
Spring/summer 2013.

1. *Jezebel* Salmon-pink
   snakeskin and lizard lace-
   up with heart cut-out and
   oversized heart lace ends.
   Spring/summer 2013.

2. *Roseum* Vintage-style colour-
   blocked heart cut-out lace-up
   with snakeskin heel and trim.
   Spring/summer 2013.

3. *Origami* 1940s-style platform
   pump with nude suede
   upper and denim-blue
   toecap, snakeskin platform
   and folded floral appliqué.
   Spring/summer 2013.

4. *Cleo* Mary Jane wooden
   platform pump with blue
   acrylic heel. In denim-blue
   suede with hexagonal buckle.
   Spring/summer 2013.

1.

2.

1. *Angora* Whimsical suede
   lilac platform pump with
   signature Parikka bunny ears,
   tapered heel and curved top-
   line. Fall/winter 2012/2013.

2. *Minnus* Cobalt-blue
   suede platform pump with
   elasticated front panel,
   lizard trim, heel and forepart
   platform. Fall/winter
   2013/2014.

3. *Roseum* Lace-up pump with
   heart cut-out and shaped
   lace-ends in cobalt-blue
   suede and brown and grey
   embossed snakeskin. Fall/
   winter 2012/2013.

4. *Julee* Fuchsia-pink T-bar
   platform sandal with
   triple-strap detailing and
   contrasting inner heel panel.
   Fall/winter 2012/2013.

3.

1.

4.

2.

3.

1. *Melt* Witty platform pump in fuchsia suede with patent leather ice cream appliqué and curved top-line. Fall/winter 2012/2013.

2. *Heeltap* Lizard mid-height platform slip-on with heel tab, exposed tongue, neon orange forepart platform and inner heel panel. Fall/winter 2012/2013.

3. *Sherbet* Fuchsia-pink mid-height suede pump with patent leather melted ice cream appliqué and heel tab. Fall/winter 2012/2013.

4. *Pfeiffer* Bunny-eared loafer with curved hourglass heel and almond toe in leopard-print ponyskin. Fall/winter 2012/2013.

Michel Perry

Cerises Cherry T-bar sandal with tapered stacked leather heel and ankle strap closure from the spring/summer 2010 look book.

Michel Perry is one of France's most revered and admired footwear designers. His whimsical shoes have a sophisticated frivolity and elegant charm. The son of a notable French shoe retailer, Perry launched his own label in 1987. His eponymous collection was met with critical acclaim and he continues to delight each and every season.

What inspired you to get into footwear design?
I have lived in the world of shoes since I was a child! My parents used to have shoe shops. I was rather indifferent at the beginning though; I wanted to be a painter. So I studied Fine Art, then one day realized I could express my creativity through shoes while at the same time meeting women – that sealed it for me.

Do you have a particular kind of woman in mind when you are designing?
I have many women in mind: a Parisian woman, at times androgynous, who embodies the persona of Parisian scamp, or epitomizes a 'couture' kind of elegance. An Englishwoman, aristocratic and bohemian, who is not afraid to shake up the status quo. A WASP from the East Coast of America, who is chic yet mischievous, her cool exterior concealing the fire within.

I generally try to appeal to a light-hearted, mischievous woman who is free-spirited and active. This woman distances herself from fashion so that she is not merely a slave to the trends. She is assured in her choices and subtle in expressing her femininity, so as not to become a caricature.

Where do you draw your inspiration from?
My imagination stems from a semi-real, semi-fantasy world, filled with images which have shaped the history of fashion and have forged iconic female figures: Jackie Kennedy, Grace Kelly, Catherine Deneuve, Blondie, Marie Antoinette. I mix my modernity with references to an idealized past. I feel a certain sense of nostalgia for a paradise lost: the French Riviera of the 1960s; winter sports of the 1950s and 60s; the London of the Stones and the Beatles; Montmartre; Hollywood.

Would you say you had a signature style? Describe it to us in five words.
Three words suffice. Know-how, frivolousness and humour. It's a brand that combines lightness with seriousness… or the other way round!

When it comes to technique and fabric, are there particular styles and materials that run through each collection?
Ahead of fabrics, for me the most important thing is the cut. The shoe is first and foremost a three-dimensional object, like a sculpture. I strive to create new lasts each season. Working on the upper is often a very simple way of highlighting the lasts even more.

How do you see the current fascination with footwear developing?
I have always maintained that the accessory is what's essential, since I founded my brand. I don't think I'm going to change now!

1. Drawings from Michel
  Perry's sketchbook.

1.

4.

2.

1. *Utopia* Cut-out peep-toe sandal in coloured python with block heel in mock crocodile skin. Spring/summer 2013.

2. *Cerises* Patchwork cherry T-bar sandal with tapered covered heel. Spring/summer 2007.

3. *Balzanes* High red ankle bootie with front-crossed buckled strap detailing and solid block heel. Fall/winter 2012/2013.

4. *Epic* Suede cowboy boot with neon-orange piping and stacked leather heel. Spring/summer 2013.

3.

1.

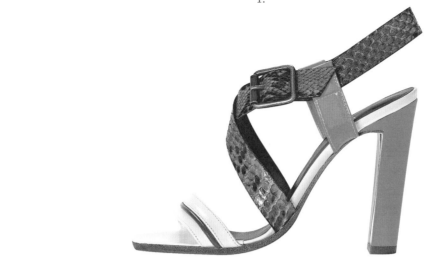

4.

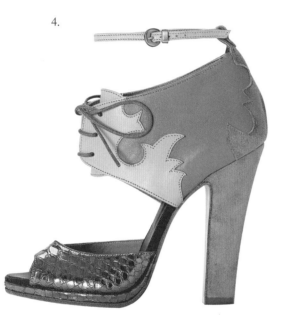

2.

1. *Odyssey* Colour-blocked
   strappy sandal in coloured
   python and calfskin, with
   buckled ankle strap and block
   heel. Spring/summer 2013.

2. *Ancre Marine* Whimsical
   anchor sandal in gold and
   white leather with blue suede
   anchor appliqué and heel.
   Spring/summer 2012.

3. *Léopoldine* Green leather
   ankle boot with half metal
   cigarette heel in gold. Spring/
   summer 2012.

4. *Allegoria 115* Lace-up cowboy
   sandal with fine buckled
   ankle strap, in metallic gold
   python, and tonal shades of
   leather and suede. Spring/
   summer 2013.

3.

1.

2.

3.

1. *Phoenix* Lace-up cowboy shoe
   with side cut-outs, petrol-
   blue python heel, and neon
   piping across the toe. Spring/
   summer 2013.

2. *Etrier* Suede knee-high boot
   in tan and black with neon-
   orange piping and solid block
   heel. Fall/winter 2012/2013.

3. *Castille* Flat T-bar sandal
   with striped panelling in
   brown and red leather and
   fine buckled ankle strap.
   Spring/summer 2012.

UNPACKING POLLINI

CELEBRATING 60 YEARS
OF CLASSIC ITALIAN FOOTWEAR AND PRESENTING THE NEW COLLECTION
FOR AUTUMN/WINTER 2013–14

Pollini

Established in 1953, Pollini has over six decades of footwear manufacturing expertise. With its roots firmly planted in the traditional production of leather goods and footwear, the heritage artisan company enjoyed a renaissance in 2010 when footwear designer extraordinaire Nicholas Kirkwood was appointed creative director.

With his signature geometric lines and flamboyant use of materials, Kirkwood has propelled Pollini footwear in a bold new direction. Drawing his creative inspiration from the richness of Pollini's extensive archive, Kirkwood has allowed himself the liberty to vary and reinterpret styles and details while preserving the brand's essence. A perfect example of this was Kirkwood's reinterpretation of the iconic 1977 Pollini 'Cavaliere' boot for fall/winter 2012/13, where he created six boots, each in the image of his ideal Pollini icons, inspired by the brand's 1970s advertising campaigns.

Today the Pollini brand is very much about clean silhouettes crafted in luxurious materials and styles, that can be worn for work or play, and are stylish yet wearable. Kirkwood has successfully injected a fashionable edge while respecting the Pollini tradition of practicality and exceptional workmanship and flair. Pollini shoes are almost completely made by hand with over 135 different stages involved in the production of each pair. It is this expertise and high-quality manufacturing that has seen the Pollini factory produce shoes for some of fashion's finest including Alberta Ferretti, Dsquared2, Moschino and Narciso Rodriguez.

Based in the Emilia-Romagna region of Italy, Pollini manufactured its first pair of shoes in 1953. The stylish yet practical sandals evoked happy times of summers on the Riviera and were a perfect fit for the changing lives of women in postwar Italy. Pollini opened its first boutique in 1963 in Ravenna, and by the 1970s had opened stores across the length and breadth of Italy, from Florence, Milan, Rome and Bologna to Parma, Verona, Bergamo and Venice.

Pollini has come a long way since its humble beginnings in the 1950s. Today it presents its collections at the international fashion weeks in Paris and Milan and has branded stores located across the globe. Pollini opened its new flagship store in 2012, situated on the prestigious Via della Spiga in the heart of Milan's fashion district. Designed by the architect Mehrnoosh Khadivi, of Craftwork Studio in London, the new minimalist concept store, with its crisp white walls and bespoke parquet flooring, is very much in keeping with the brand's new-found aesthetic.

To celebrate its sixtieth anniversary in 2013, Pollini hosted the exhibition 'Unpacking Pollini' during Milan Fashion Week. Sixty archive pieces sat alongside new styles from the fall/winter 2013/14 collection in an installation that showcased six decades of the brand's contribution to fashion from both a historic and contemporary perspective.

1.

2.

4.

3.

1. Grey suede platform lace-up with neon-orange Aztec-inspired appliquéd platform, binding and laces. Fall/winter 2012.

2. Grey suede pump with neon-orange binding, stiletto heel and super-fine cross-over straps. Fall/winter 2012.

3. Black ridged platform pump with silver metallic toecap and block heel. Fall/winter 2012.

4. Lucite wedge heel in silver grey moiré leather with pointed toe and super-fine buckled ankle strap. Fall/winter 2012.

1.

2.

4.

3.

1. Fishtail platform pump in black with contrasting cobalt-blue forepart platform and heel and shock neon-yellow lining. Fall/winter 2012.

2. Cobalt and black Aztec-inspired graphic sandal with multi-strap detailing and back zip closure. Fall/winter 2012.

3. Androgynous laceless slip-on, in orange and grey variations. Fall/winter 2012.

4. Cobalt-blue suede lace-up with ridged cleated sole and stacked leather heel. Fall/winter 2012.

1.

4.

2.

3.

1. Burnt orange metallic pointed slingback with harlequin heel. Fall/winter 2013.

2. Green crocodile knee-high boot with stacked leather heel (a reinterpretation of Pollini's 1977 Cavaliere boot). Fall/winter 2013.

3. Orange patent loafer with pointed toe, mid-height covered heel and contrast blue trim. Fall/winter 2013.

4. Grey suede mid-height platform pump with neon orange sole and inside heel panel. Fall/winter 2013.

1.

4.

2.

3.

1. Pointed grey suede loafer with neon-orange trim and covered stiletto heel. Fall/winter 2013.

2. Embroidered peep-toe bootie with Lucite wedge heel and back zip closure. Fall/winter 2013.

3. Grey and grape loafer bootie with covered mid-height heel and metal detailing. Fall/winter 2013.

4. Blue patent platform ankle boot with pointed toe and neon-orange sole and inside heel panel. Fall/winter 2013.

Prada

A Geisha-like sandal is modernized with a heavy embellished sole in silver. The strappy upper is made of delicate oyster-pink satin with bows across the front. Spring/summer 2013.

The origins of the Prada group can be traced back to 1913, when Mario Prada, the grandfather of Miuccia Prada, founded the brand. Not unlike Louis Vuitton, Prada's foundations were laid in the luggage, handbags and leather accessories industry. The key to their success was exclusivity – sophisticated techniques and materials applied to quality pieces which were sold in the Prada store at the prestigious glass-covered Galleria Vittorio Emanuele II arcade in Milan. Prada offered a kind of luxury that was quickly recognized by the European aristocracy; where Prada today can be found on the arms or feet of fashion's elite, the Prada of yesteryear held a royal status. In 1919 Prada was appointed an official supplier to the Italian royal household and incorporated the House of Savoy's coat of arms and knotted rope design into its logo.

It was in the late 1970s that Prada started to become the label we know today. The collaboration between husband and wife Miuccia Prada and Patrizio Bertelli took the brand into the international fashion arena. Prada's history of producing luxurious and quality items is continued today and across all corners of the high-end fashion market. As well as its instantly recognizable footwear collection, the Prada brand includes men's and women's leather goods, and ready-to-wear clothing. Together with Miuccia Prada's unique vision and famed ability to create trends rather than follow them, the brand continues to be at the forefront of fashion, season upon season.

Every shoe within Prada's footwear collections can rightly be called a piece of art, and each season Miuccia Prada keeps the fashion cognoscenti and dedicated customer guessing as to which direction the collection will take. Neither has ever guessed correctly. Miuccia's ability to take inspiration from past decades and modernize them is another way in which she taps into the zeitgeist.

The juxtaposition between her spring/summer 2012 and fall/winter 2012/13 collections was no exception to the rule. Where spring/summer drew influences from the glamour of the 1950s, with flames appliquéd onto delicate sandals, fall/winter 2012/13 saw an altogether heavier silhouette, featuring blunt masculine styles and 1940s-style platforms with thick straps. Appliquéd flowers and heavy beading were combined with silhouettes reminiscent of the 1970s. Heavy platforms and fluted heels were juxtaposed with daisy-like flowers usually associated with a 1960s vibe. Miuccia literally kept the fashion world on its toes.

What makes Prada such a continuously visionary brand is this ability to swap and change direction each season, while still retaining its sense of brand. As Miuccia said of the fall/winter 2012/13 collection, 'Everyone has a theory about their collections these days, but I'm sick of theory. This collection is about the *pleasure* of fashion.'

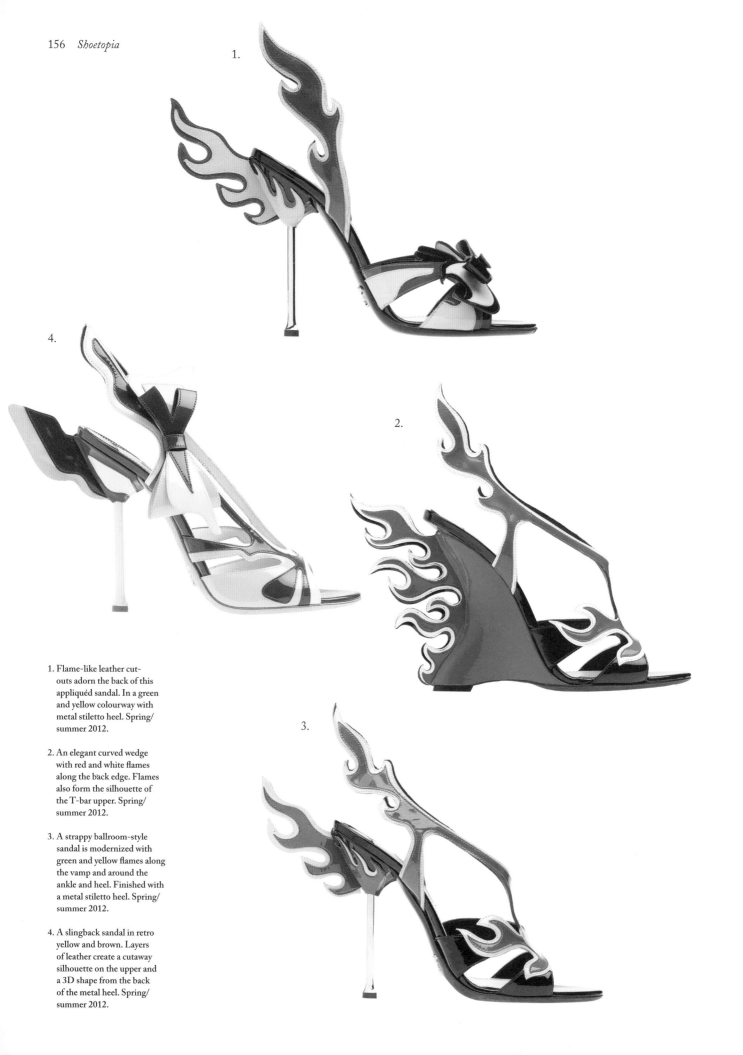

1.

4.

2.

3.

1. Flame-like leather cut-outs adorn the back of this appliquéd sandal. In a green and yellow colourway with metal stiletto heel. Spring/summer 2012.

2. An elegant curved wedge with red and white flames along the back edge. Flames also form the silhouette of the T-bar upper. Spring/summer 2012.

3. A strappy ballroom-style sandal is modernized with green and yellow flames along the vamp and around the ankle and heel. Finished with a metal stiletto heel. Spring/summer 2012.

4. A slingback sandal in retro yellow and brown. Layers of leather create a cutaway silhouette on the upper and a 3D shape from the back of the metal heel. Spring/summer 2012.

1.

2.

1. A simple black Oxford with
chunky sole is dipped into
rubber to create a plasticized
effect on the upper and sole.
In brown/black and red/black
colourways. Fall/winter 2012.

2. Simple black Oxfords are
scattered with appliquéd
flowers, creating a retro hippy
look. Fall/winter 2012.

3.

1.

2.

1. A powder-blue chunky
   platform sandal with ankle
   strap. The appliquéd flowers
   that run through this
   collection are seen in red and
   blue. Fall/winter 2012.

2. A mustard-yellow high-cut
   pump with criss-cross strap
   detailing. Oversized plastic
   gems and beads are scattered
   over the vamp and platform
   sole. Fall/winter 2012.

3. A chunky high-cut pump
   with criss-cross strap
   detailing. Featuring
   appliquéd flowers in red
   and white all over the
   upper. Fall/winter 2012.

1.

2.

3.

1. A chunky-heeled sandal with
   bow detail is modernized
   with a leather sock attached
   from the ankle upwards. In
   olive green and black. Spring/
   summer 2013.

2. A Geisha-like wedge sandal
   in royal blue featuring white
   Japanese-style flowers along
   the sole and bow detail on the
   straps. Spring/summer 2013.

3. Red satin Geisha sandal
   with cut-out detailing in
   the sculptural wedge, and
   featuring bow detail on the
   straps. Spring/summer 2013.

Alain Quilici

Whippet A pointed black pump is embellished with an ornate silver heel sculpted into an elegant dog. Fall/winter 2012/2013.

Alain Quilici has only been established since 2007, but his aesthetic is fast becoming recognizable among those in the know. For Quilici, footwear is in the blood. Coming from a family of Tuscan-born shoemakers, Quilici has a unique approach to design: 'form follows function follows VISION.'

His inspiration is diverse; he cites 'the flesh and metal hybrids of Shinya Tsukamoto's post-human cinema, the physical and psychological deformations of David Cronenberg's movies and the muscular drama of Francis Bacon's and Egon Schiele's paintings' as just some of the ideas he looks to when designing his collection.

Quilici's inspirations are apparent in a pared-down colour palette that is generally limited to black and white, grey and flesh tones. The form of his shoes also follows this rigorous and austere approach. Not one to sacrifice his integrity for fashion trends and fads, his silhouettes are 'often quizzing, always incisive, never frivolous.'

What inspired you to get into footwear design?
I have always felt the need to 'mould' concepts or feelings in concrete terms. From the beginning, footwear became this vehicle for me. Throughout my education I have been fascinated by the duality, the dream, the metamorphosis, and above all the mechanical transformation of the human body. These were the main ideas that shaped my perception of the world; I am attracted by anything that has a sad, decadent and melancholic spirit within. 'Transformation', or the visionary representation of the truth, is the essence of my job.

Do you have a particular kind of woman in mind when you are designing?
Actually none in particular, but I like to think that the women wearing my shoes have a really personal relationship with them, wearing them as a real extension of their bodies.

Where do you draw your inspiration from?
I'm very inspired by industrial design.

Would you say you had a signature style? Describe it to us in five words.
Parallelism, geometries, scars, metal and mutation.

When it comes to technique and fabric, are there particular styles and materials that run through each collection?
Wood is a material present in every collection. I'm fascinated by its limits and its qualities, and each time I like to discover more. It has a really interesting ductility.

How do you see the current fascination with footwear developing?
There is now an ability to 'redefine' the way shoes look, moving away from the stereotyped shape of footwear.

What are your ambitions for your brand in the future?
To build a personal and recognizable aesthetic.

1.

2.

4.

3.

1. *Victoria* A sculptural sandal in ecru and black with high chunky heel covered in rubberized green plastic. Green handstitching features on the footbed. Spring/summer 2013.

2. *Fiona* A deconstructed lace-up ankle boot, with peep toe, in rough natural leather. The conical heel features zigzag cut-outs on the back. Spring/summer 2013.

3. *Samantha* A sculptural sandal in camel and white with high chunky heel covered in rubberized camel plastic. Camel handstitching features on the footbed. Spring/summer 2013.

4. *Samantha* The same style with the heel covered in rubberized red plastic, and red handstitching on the footbed. Spring/summer 2013.

1.

2.

4.

3.

1. *Tazi* A black mesh pointed ankle boot featuring a dog carved into a silver heel. Fall/winter 2012.

2. *Whippet* A royal-blue pointed pump with extended tongue and strap detailing. A sculptural dog is cut into the white heel. Fall/winter 2012.

3. *Jordan* A peep-toe, lace-up ankle boot with a wooden sculpted heel, which is attached to the platform hybrid sole. Spring/summer 2013.

4. *April* A white ankle boot with multi-strap vamp. The concealed platform in metallic leather is revealed at the front. Spring/summer 2013.

Anastasia Radevich

'Kinetic' collection (2011); ankle boot with sculptural wire heel and platform in galvanized black metal (top). 'Lost Civilizations' collection (2012); a textural ankle boot in metallic finished with cutaway wedge spelling 'This will destroy you' in metal (below).

A Canadian of Belarusian origin, Anastasia Radevich honed her craft while studying for a diploma at the prestigious London College of Fashion, as well as stints at design houses Alexander McQueen and Nicholas Kirkwood. Living and working in Montreal, her collections – the first in 2009 - are eclectic and a true reflection of Radevich's personality. Referring to herself as a 'shoe artist' rather than a designer, what drives Radevich is free, unobstructed expression and creativity. Her approach to design, which is to treat a shoe as a canvas, is easy to see in her creations. Her shoes are compelling sculptural objects that tell a story, as well as making a statement.

The collection featured here, 'Lost Civilizations', is a true representation of her aesthetic with a focus entirely on materials and structure. While the upper construction remains fairly simple, the leathers are painted and treated until they become unrecognizable from their original state. The heels are seemingly made from found objects and industrial materials to form words and messages. The overall effect is bordering on science fiction.

What inspired you to get into footwear design?
I grew up in a family of three generations of shoemakers and have been helping to make shoes since childhood. As I grew up I wanted to express certain feelings and ideas and have chosen shoes as a tool, because I know this craft very well. Shoes became my 'canvas'.

Do you have a particular kind of woman in mind when you are designing?
A free spirited and adventurous character.

Where do you draw your inspiration from?
Nature and philosophy.

Would you say you had a signature style? Describe it to us in five words.
It is a blend of biology + dreams + freedom + energy + inspiration (i.e. the shoe has to inspire people). The energy is feminine at this point, but I plan to include a masculine approach in a future collection.

When it comes to technique and fabric, are there particular styles and materials that run through each collection?
So far it has been silk prints and embroidery.

How do you see the current fascination with footwear developing?
The sky is the limit. There are two major directions: heritage, i.e. going back to bespoke shoes and traditional cuts, or going forward, i.e. experimenting with shapes and materials and sometimes even combining these two directions into one.

What are your ambitions for your brand in the future?
To continue to express ideas through shoes, and have a bigger audience to understand those ideas. Also to launch a ready-to-wear line with totally different aesthetics.

1. Rusted leather round-toe pump with fossil-effect platform heel. 'Lost Civilizations' collection, 2012.

2. Metallic silver round-toe pump with moulded, pearlized, sci-fi effect platform heel. 'Lost Civilizations' collection, 2012.

3. Ankle boot with appliquéd fabric ruffles in dove grey, featuring a matt-black sculptural heel and platform. 'Dreamfall' collection, 2011.

1.

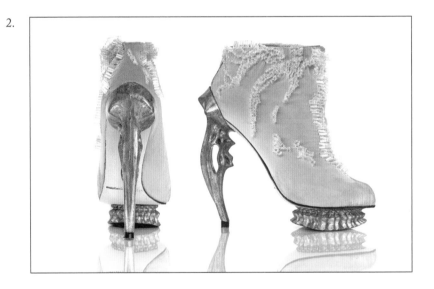

2.

3.

1. Plain pointed ankle boot
   with high-rise wedge. The
   words 'This will destroy you'
   are carved out of the metal
   sole. 'Lost Civilizations'
   collection, 2012.

2. Dove-grey satin ankle boot
   with intricate embroidery
   detailing. The sculptural sole
   and heel are in silver metal.
   'Dreamfall' collection, 2011.

3. Leather ankle boot with
   ombre painted-effect upper
   and white fossilized sole
   detail. 'Lost Civilizations'
   collection, 2012.

1. Round-toe pump with
   mutated wedge sole detail,
   all finished in a white, tactile,
   dustlike powder effect. 'Lost
   Civilizations' collection, 2012.

1.

2.

3.

1. Bronzed leather T-bar sandal with multi-strap detailing, and oxidized metal sculptural heel and platform. 'Kinetic' collection, 2011.

2. Ankle boot with appliquéd fabric ruffles in beige, featuring a matt-black sculptural heel and platform. 'Dreamfall' collection, 2011.

3. 'Dreamfall' collection, 2011.

Eugène Riconneaus

Cara Pastel-blue suede sandal with wraparound ankle strap and notched leather sole. Spring/summer 2012.

It is easy to trace the roots of Eugène Riconneaus's designs back to his training with a traditional French bootmaker and also the master shoemakers of Northampton in England. His elegant and feminine designs for spring/summer 2012 combined traditional techniques and finishing touches such as notching and tasselled laces with an edgy fashionability aimed at the modern woman. Leathers and suedes in neutral colours of tan, beige and cornflower blue were used on the uppers of 1940s-style sandals and vulcanized sneakers to create an essential capsule collection. The label started producing capsule collections in 2009, and since 2012 Eugène Riconneaus has made 30 styles each season.

What inspired you to get into footwear design?
This is related to my childhood. I was born with a skateboard under my feet. As a boy I was sponsored and took part in skate contests. But I wore my shoes out too quickly, which annoyed my parents. So I learned to mend them with a bootmaker at the corner of my street. He taught me everything, I spent a lot of time there, much more than I spent at school. My life then divided between the shoemaker's shop and skating. Until one day, when I was still very young, I discovered women. The rest is history…

Do you have a particular kind of woman in mind when you are designing?
I'm not narrow-minded enough to stick to just one woman. I meet the Eugène Riconneaus woman every day.

Where do you draw your inspiration from?
Women.

Would you say you had a signature style?
My signature is linked to technical knowledge: tassels, braided leather, notched edging. It is also linked to skate culture: leopard, checks, mad prints.

Describe it to us in five words.
Ambiguous, radical, perfectionist, charmer, chameleon.

When it comes to technique and fabric, are there particular styles and materials that run through each collection?
My signature style is found in all my collections. From a technical point of view, I use materials like kid velvet, feathers, lambskin, ponyskin.

How do you see the current fascination with footwear developing?
Women don't show off the shoes they wear so much as shoes show off the women who wear them. A personality can change dramatically just by wearing a pair of shoes because they are a self-sufficient design, thanks to their three dimensions. The fascination also comes from the fact that the woman wearing the shoe doesn't just wear it, she enhances it.

What are your ambitions for your brand in the future?
To send a shoe to the moon.

1.

2.

3.

1. *Nicole* White calfskin sneaker
   with patent black calfskin
   detailing and blake sole.
   Spring/summer 2012.

2. *Sky* Natural calfskin mule
   with contrasting black leather
   heel and bow trim on the
   upper. Spring/summer 2012.

3. *Anna* Peep-toe platform
   pump in natural and black
   calfskin, featuring notched
   leather sole. Spring/
   summer 2012.

1.

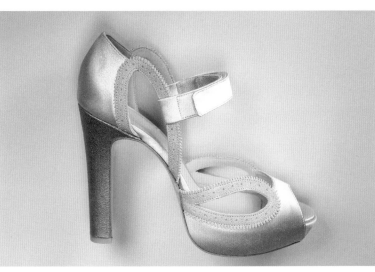

4.

2.

1. *'Secret Name'* Cutaway T-bar style with patent leather trim and covered slimline wedge. Spring/summer 2013.

2. *Di Calypso* Platform sandal with wide ankle strap. With a textured black leather upper and notched leather sole detail. Spring/summer 2013.

3. *Nina* Asymmetric pointed pump in powder-pink satin and calfskin. Spring/summer 2013.

4. *Lizzie* Retro platform sandal in dove-grey satin with neon-green leather brogued trim. Spring/summer 2013.

3.

Park Glamorous glitter and nude leather caged sandal, worn by Roxane Mesquida for the spring 2012 campaign, photographed by Mary Rozzi.

A designer whose shoes have graced the feet of some of Hollywood's most glamorous leading ladies, Canadian-born Rousseau studied footwear design at Cordwainers in London before fine-tuning his skills working alongside the likes of Matthew Williamson, Isabella Fiore and John Richmond. He went it alone in 2008 with the launch of his fall/winter collection.

What inspired you to get into footwear design?
I grew up in the north of Quebec. MTV was my escape; it was my way to travel and discover cultures and fashion from around the world. I first started drawing shoes as a teenager after watching the Deee-Lite 'Groove is in the Heart' video. I was influenced by its unique styling, but it was the overstated retro footwear that first caught my attention.

Do you have a particular kind of woman in mind when you are designing?
The muse of the label is young French actress Roxane Mesquida. She embodies the effortless beauty, elegance and style I want to portray in my work. She also happens to be a good friend of the label and the face of our spring 2012 campaign.

Where do you draw your inspiration from?
It varies every season, but generally I'm inspired by art, design, nature, music, nightlife and travel; it is something that constantly changes and evolves. I like to have a clear direction in my collections and it is important that my inspirations are reflected in the final designs.

Would you say you had a signature style? Describe it to us in five words.
The 'Aizza' pump is one of our signature silhouettes with its distinctive chiselled toe shape and killer stiletto. In five words it's fierce, distinctive, sensual, sharp and feminine.

When it comes to technique and fabric, are there particular styles and materials that run through each collection?
I love working with glitter, it's become a signature for the label mixed with natural leather trims. I also love kid suede because it takes on colour in rich saturated ways; I often use it to create colour-blocking in the collection. I've also been working with silk satin for similar reasons.

How do you see the current fascination with footwear developing?
Shoes have become the key object of seduction in recent years. There continues to be wild creativity in shoe design and customers really respond to that. Women have learned to use footwear to express different sides of their personalities. Regardless of age, women now take serious risks with their choice of footwear.

What are your ambitions for your brand in the future?
I want to continue to offer compelling collections season after season while increasing the exposure of the label in various countries. I look forward to opening the first Jerome C. Rousseau flagship store; it will allow us to display the full collection and illustrate the story behind each season.

1.

4.

2.

3.

1. *Aizza* Jerome C. Rousseau's signature pump with soft rounded toe, fin-shaped top-line and 11.5 cm (4¾in) stiletto heel. Fall/winter 2013/2014.

2. *Bryant* Poppy-red peep-toe pump with Rousseau's signature sculptural thorn heel, in luxury suede. Fall/winter 2013/2014.

3. *Dragonette Multi* Jerome C. Rousseau's anniversary colour-blocked T-bar pump with metallic gold leather piping and contrasting toecap. Fall/winter 2013/2014.

4. *Arcos* Multi-strap wedge sandal with rich metal double-zip front opening and natural python-skin upper. Spring/summer 2013.

1.

4.

2.

1. *Elli* Peep-toe bootie in monochrome houndstooth ponyskin and black patent leather trim heel. Fall/winter 2012/2013.

2. *Juda* Dramatic floral-printed velvet peep-toe ankle boot with contrasting metallic gold glitter heel. Fall/winter 2013/2014.

3. *Simkes* A satin, colour-blocked modern patch-worked sandal with crinkle metallic leather trim, graphic cut-outs and exposed back zip closure. Fall/winter 2012/2013.

4. *Sibi* Half D'Orsay peep-toe bootie with super-high covered stiletto heel in vivid purple suede. Fall/winter 2013/2014.

3.

1.

4.

2.

3.

1. *Lund T* Modern gladiator-style sandal featuring an extended ankle strap with graphic stitch lines, in soft gold metallic leather and suede. Spring/summer 2013.

2. *Jiro* Black and tan leather stiletto boot with pointed toe and intricate bondage-style straps across the back. Fall/winter 2013/2014.

3. *Popp* Minimalist silver metallic sandal with delicate cross-over ankle strap. Fall/winter 2013/2014.

4. *Juda* Peep-toe ankle boot in metallic rose-gold basketweave leather and gold leather heel. Spring/summer 2013.

5. The fall/winter 2013/2014 collection on display at the designer's studio.

5.

Rupert Sanderson

Rupert Sanderson

Flamante Platform sandal with pink starburst appliqué and fuchsia-pink stiletto heel. Spring/summer 2012 look book.

Rupert Sanderson's shoes are the height of elegance; refined and sophisticated, they have a timeless quality and are designed to flatter and lengthen the leg and make the women who wear them feel sexy.

Adopting the 'less is more' approach to design, Sanderson purposely avoids fussy hardware and over-decorating the foot, instead focusing on the three fundamental elements of design: cut, silhouette and material. Indeed it is these three ingredients that are the starting point for each new collection, whether it is the sensual curve and silhouette of the lasts and heels or the highest quality and finish of leathers and fabrics.

With two UK stores located in London's finest retail districts, Mayfair and Knightsbridge, it is no surprise that Sanderson has built up a huge clientele among the rich and famous. Kate Moss, Gwyneth Paltrow, Freida Pinto, Keira Knightley and Kate Middleton are all big fans.

Sanderson's success is a great achievement for someone whose interest in footwear design came quite late. After an unsuccessful career in advertising, Sanderson decided to study at the world-renowned Cordwainers College in London. Such was his passion that during the summer break of his two-year course he rode to Italy on his motorbike and set about visiting as many shoe factories, tanneries and last makers as possible.

Shortly after graduating, Sanderson returned to Italy, where he worked for two of Italy's most revered footwear companies, Sergio Rossi and Bruno Magli. 'I feel proud to have been able to work with the founders, and their families, of both these companies before they were bought by larger

luxury goods companies,' explains Sanderson. It proved an invaluable experience and introduced him to the close-knit Italian footwear manufacturing community, ultimately allowing him to realize his own dream in 2001.

Sanderson's continuing success is perhaps due in part to his obsessive passion for the Italian craft of shoemaking. In order to maintain his relationship with the factory he has been using since his first collection, Sanderson decided to buy a controlling interest in it to safeguard the skill and know-how built up over generations of shoemakers. In so doing he has ensured that every pair of Rupert Sanderson shoes are the best they could possibly be.

In 2008 he founded the Fashion Fringe Shoes initiative with renowned fashion commentator Colin McDowell, with the aim of discovering and nurturing new design talent. He has himself been awarded the British Fashion Council's Accessory Designer of the Year in 2008 and the same at the *Elle* Style Awards in 2009.

Since 2009 Sanderson has designed the shoes for Karl Lagerfeld's main line collection and is set to collaborate with the likes of young designers Maxime Simoens and Osman Yousefzada. He continues to grow his retail empire with stores located in the UK, Hong Kong and Paris.

1.

2.

4.

3.

1. *Alroi* Blue and black graphic pump with cobalt-blue stripe running down the quarters and looping on the toe. Fall/winter 2012/2013.

2. *Estelle* Jagged cut-out sandal in black calf leather with stiletto heel and back zip closure. Classic collection.

3. *Garron* Blue suede ankle boot with hidden platform and stiletto heel with graphic cobalt-blue stripe detailing. Fall/winter 2012/2013.

4. *Troy* Perfectly proportioned nude patent leather stiletto pump. Classic collection.

1.

4.

2.

3.

1. *Pasha* Black leather ankle
   boot with covered block heel
   and buckled strap detailing.
   Fall/winter 2012/2013.

2. *Pomp* Gold and black laser-
   cut suede and satin butterfly
   platform pump inspired by
   the Marquise de Pompadour.
   Fall/winter 2012/2013.

3. *Harper* Elegant platform
   pump in purple patent
   leather with covered forepart
   platform and towering
   stiletto heel. Fall/winter
   2012/2013.

4. *Jussy* Red cowboy wedge
   bootie in Pampa kid leather,
   with black and gold crossed
   guns and floral embroidery.
   Fall/winter 2012/2013.

1.

2.

1. *Mist* Gold leather stiletto
   sandal with crossed toe
   straps, crossed elasticated
   ankle straps and covered heel.
   Spring/summer 2012.

2. *Marilyn* Evening platform
   sandal designed in homage to
   Marilyn Monroe. In glitter
   leather with gold beaded
   lip appliqué. Fall/winter
   2012/2013.

1. *Kalit* Super-high wedge,
  T-bar sandal in white canvas
  and patent leather. Spring/
  summer 2012.

Rupert Sanderson

Camilla Skovgaard

Bridge Wedge Black heel-less boot with exaggerated cut-out platform and fin-shaped top-line. Fall/winter 2012/2013 look book.

Danish-born designer Camilla Skovgaard is renowned for her innovative footwear collections, first launched in 2006. Her shoes, often recognizable by their sawtooth sole, constantly drive forward the possibilities of footwear design. Inspired by her love of architecture and sinister gothic landscapes, her distinctive avant-garde aesthetic focuses on form, material and style over embellishment and ornamentation.

What inspired you to get into footwear design?
When I lived in Dubai designing gowns for the Sheikh's wives and daughters, I noticed that shoes were often an afterthought. I read an article about Cordwainers, hid it in my drawer, and when I was ready for the next step in my career I applied and attended. I loved learning the craft of shoemaking – a very different process to clothing.

Do you have a particular kind of woman in mind when you are designing?
Not really. I design what I feel. You could say I'm designing for women who don't want to look like a colourful fruitcake when they go out; I tend to have a starker palette and more harrowing aesthetic. I still want to click some serious high heels about town – just on my own terms.

Where do you draw your inspiration from?
I don't work from a specific 'inspiration' or mood board; I design mainly from the gut. To be honest most of my designs start as scribbles on small yellow Post-it notes.

Would you say you had a signature style? Describe it to us in five words.
Pared-down detailing, intellectual sophistication. Unconventional shaping with architecturally inspired treads are at the fore… and I don't seem to be able to stay away from hairs and drapes that drag along the floor for more than a couple of seasons. It started with human hair in 2007.

When it comes to technique and fabric, are there particular styles and materials that run through each collection?
I have become known for the rubber saw-sole which is patented in over seven countries. At the end of each season the basic wedge with the saw-sole is offered as well as an updated version such as the one tooth for fall/winter 2011 and the heel-less wedge for spring/summer 2013. It's important to build on what is successful season on season, but to make it new and fresh.

How do you see the current fascination with footwear developing?
I think the sky's the limit with shoes but I will remain true to who I am as a designer. With shoes you can update an entire look from day to evening, or even from one season to the next, so it's not surprising that women spend so much money on good shoes.

What are your ambitions for your brand in the future?
I am working on developing the men's collection as well as a handbag collection. I will also be launching an online store, hopefully followed by a London flagship store.

1.

4.

2.

3.

1. *Flame* Indigo slingback stiletto sandal with fin-shaped straps, stiletto heel and sawtooth rubber sole. Spring/summer 2012/2013.

2. *Prey* Sculptural slingback stiletto sandal in tan leather with extended front panelling. Resort 2013.

3. *Ankle Wedge* Wedge bootie with exaggerated rubber sawtooth sole, in brush-stroke leather. Resort 2013.

4. *Prey* Black and white sculptural slingback stiletto sandal with extended front panelling. Resort 2013.

1.

2.

4.

3.

1. *Moon Wedge* Rounded wedge ankle boot with exaggerated sawtooth sole. Spring/summer 2013.

2. *Indochine* Suede and leather wedge sandal with cut-out strap detailing and wide ankle cuff with back zip closure. Spring/summer 2013.

3. *Heel-less Sandal* Gold heel-less strappy sandal with ankle cuff and back zip closure, forepart platform and exaggerated sawtooth rubber sole. Spring/summer 2013.

4. *Heel-less Bar Strap Sandal* Black heel-less sandal with exaggerated sawtooth rubber sole and back zip fastening. Spring/summer 2013.

1.

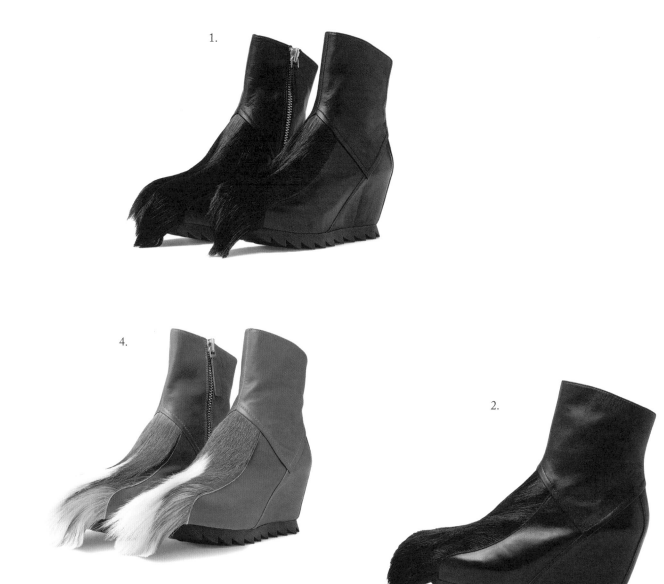

4.

2.

3.

1. *Fur Sweeper Boot* Black wedge
   ankle boot with ponyskin toe
   trim and rubber sawtooth
   sole. Fall/winter 2012/2013.

2. Lateral view of 1.

3. *Ankle Wedge* Black
   leather wedge bootie with
   exaggerated rubber sawtooth
   sole. Available every season.

4. *Fur Sweeper Boot* Brown
   wedge ankle boot with
   natural-coloured ponyskin
   toe trim and black rubber
   sawtooth sole. Fall/winter
   2012/2013.

1.

2.

4.

3.

1. *Prey Bootie* Black sculptural peep-toe stiletto bootie with scooped top-line and back zip closure. Resort 2013.

2. *Cage Leg Sandal* Black platform stiletto bootie with graphic cut-outs on the ankle panel. Resort 2013.

3. *Bridge Wedge* Black heel-less boot with exaggerated cut-out platform and fin-shaped top-line. Fall/winter 2012/2013.

4. *Trashbag Boot* Black leather platform boot with raw-edge leather funnel-shaped cuff. Pre-fall 2012.

LD Tuttle

The Lost Knee-length black suede boot with chunky heel. Fall/winter 2012.

Tiffany Tuttle founded LD Tuttle in 2006 with her husband and business partner, Richard Lidinsky. Before the launch she studied at the Fashion Institute of Technology, and went on to receive a further degree in fashion design, honing her couture craft with big design houses Givenchy and Rebecca Taylor. The close link between fashion design and shoe design remains important within the LD Tuttle brand. The designer has collaborated with Peter Pilotto and Nicole and Michael Colovos to create exclusive catwalk collections.

What inspired you to get into footwear design?
It was just a basic love of shoes. I love that shoes are something small that you can hold in your hands and study all dimensions of. One day I decided to leave clothing design and go on a footwear program in Italy, and after that I launched my own collection.

Do you have a particular kind of woman in mind when you are designing?
I think of the women I know – my friends and family. I want to create shoes that they can use every day and that can become a part of them. I love seeing how different people incorporate the collection into their wardrobe, how the shoes themselves change as they are worn.

Where do you draw your inspiration from?
I draw inspiration from art, films, images around me and books. It can be the mood of a particular novel that inspires me, or a moment in history, or a concept that I have just read about. The spring/ summer 2013 collection 'Ambulamus' was inspired by the sense of isolation and empty, haunted spaces that are present in the work of Alberto Giacometti and *Death in Venice* by Thomas Mann.

Would you say you had a signature style? Describe it to us in five words.
Raw and spare, utilitarian, romantic, unvarnished.

When it comes to technique and fabric, are there particular styles and materials that run through each collection?
I design by draping the shoes on a foot or last. To do this, I use very soft, thin leathers, often unlined. I then create different support structures hidden under the draping to hold the foot and support the shoe. I like to play with movement and change, so often the shape is something that can be altered by the wearer – a boot can be folded down, unzipped or a snap left undone to show a different shape.

How do you see the current fascination with footwear developing?
In the last few years there has been a lot of fetishization of contemporary culture in general, including shoes. As people have become more interested in footwear, designers have really pushed their visions.

What are your ambitions for your brand in the future?
I would like to add a men's collection. I also plan to expand into small leather goods. Most importantly, I want to continue to build on the collection that I have, creating more shoes for our customers within our specific aesthetic.

1.

2.

4.

1. *The Vapor* Collapsed ankle boot in soft neutral nubuck. Features a side zip closure with peep toe and chunky Cuban-esque heel. Spring/summer 2013.

2. *The Whisper* A round-toe pump in soft neutral nubuck with chunky heel and multicoloured feather trim. Fall/winter 2012.

3. *The Ruin* Grey suede multi-strap shoe/sandal hybrid with concealed wedge detail. Spring/summer 2013.

4. *The Lounge* Soft black leather ankle boot with exposed heel and wraparound ankle strap feature. Spring/summer 2012.

3.

1.

4.

2.

3.

1. *The Spiral* Demi wedge style in cobalt-blue and natural snakeskin, featuring wide straps wrapped over the EVA sole. Fall/winter 2012.

2. *The Mesh* A black and emerald chunky multi-strap shoe with a Cuban-style heel. Featuring ponyskin and snakeskin leathers. Fall/winter 2012.

3. *The Fade* A high-heeled platform sandal with multiple straps in emerald leather and snakeskin. Fall/winter 2012.

4. *The Freeze* A knotted upper forms the vamp of this delicate sandal. The cut-out wedge adds an avant-garde touch. Spring/summer 2013.

Louis Vuitton

A chequerboard print in traditional monochrome covers the whole of this kitten-heel pump with bow adornment. Spring/summer 2013.

With a brand as steeped in history as Louis Vuitton, it would be easy to fall into the trap of solely producing classic designs for a loyal customer base. Louis Vuitton might have succumbed, but their appointment of fashion rebel Marc Jacobs as creative director pointed the brand in an entirely different direction.

To understand the design philosophy that Jacobs has taken and adapted to bring the brand into the twenty-first century is to delve into the company's origins. The French fashion house's story began in 1854 when Louis Vuitton Malletier set out as a designer and maker of practical, high-quality trunks that were, importantly, stackable. In 1872 a beige and red stripe canvas design was introduced; quickly becoming popular with the Paris elite, it announced the brand as a luxury item.

When Vuitton passed away in 1892, the reins were handed over to his son Georges Vuitton, who went on to grow the house into a worldwide corporation. The LV Monogram canvas, created in 1896 to prevent counterfeit, is considered the first example of branding. It was only in 1959, when a supple version of the original Monogram canvas was produced using new technology, that the company branched out into purses, bags and wallets.

Today the very same patterns can be seen across the collection, but this time in the hands of legendary New York designer Marc Jacobs. Appointed in 1997, Jacobs swiftly expanded the house's offering to include clothing as well as footwear. His collaborations with artists from Stephen Sprouse to

Takashi Murakami ensured that the Louis Vuitton brand remained in the spotlight and moved with the times by appealing to customers both old and new.

Jacobs's eclectic approach to the footwear range manages to encapsulate the history of the house while retaining an air of elegance and fashionability. Traditional fabrics are constantly juxtaposed with modern silhouettes, and vice versa. The classic Damier check was reinterpreted in a fresh new lemon zest colourway across a classic 1960s pump for spring/summer 2013 – a style that will appeal equally to the latest fashionista as it will to the original LV customer. A 1950s peep-toe pump gets a modern-day twist with an oversized fur pom-pom and diamanté-encrusted heel, while elsewhere, a classic Chelsea boot is sexed up in patent leather with a subversive pointed toe (both pre-fall 2013).

With Jacobs's legacy, new creative director Nicolas Ghesquière and the rich history of the brand, Louis Vuitton is determined to maintain its status as the most sought-after luxury brand in the world.

1. The Damier check is reinterpreted in a fresh lemon zest and white colourway across a classic 1960s-style pump with metallic rectangular block heel. Spring/summer 2013.

2. Peep-toe pump in sensual red leather with a fur pompom trim on the vamp and diamanté-encrusted heel. Pre-fall 2013.

3. Slingback 1960s-style pump with elongated toe in caramel kid leather. A block heel in white modernizes the style. Spring/summer 2013.

4. A classic brown and cream colourway in traditional Damier check fabric. Spring/summer 2013.

1.

4.

2.

3.

1. Vampish pump with V-cut topline in red suede and black sculpted heel. The ankle strap is a wide black ribbon. Pre-fall 2013.

2. Low-cut pump with V-cut topline detail in striking red kid. A thin strap in the same leather draws attention to the ankle. Pre-fall 2013.

3. Elegant ankle boot in contrasting red and black leathers. The high-shine kid leather on the ankle makes a striking graphic shape. Pre-fall 2013.

4. Retro slingback in an asymmetric colour combination of lemon and white. Spring/summer 2013.

1.

2.

4.

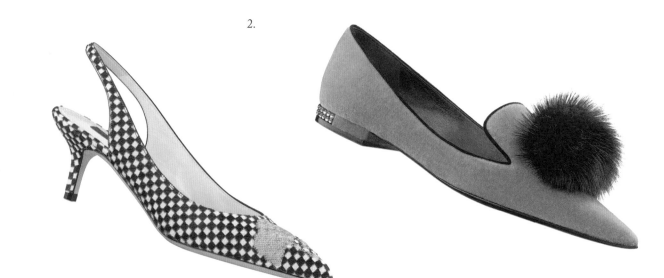

3.

1. A simple black pump is given an evening slant with a diamanté-encrusted kitten heel and V-cut vamp. Pre-fall 2013.

2. Simple slipper style in mink suede with an oversized fur pompom on the vamp and a flash of diamanté across the flat heel. Pre-fall 2013.

3. Classic slingback with stiletto heel, in vivid green. A geometric adornment on the vamp features a white floral silhouette. Spring/summer 2013.

4. Damier fabric covers the upper and heel of this simple kitten-heel slingback, with a fabric bow in zesty lemon across the vamp. Spring/summer 2013.

1.

2.

4.

1. A classic kitten-heel pump in deepest chocolate-brown fabric. A white floral silhouette adorns the upper. Spring/summer 2013.

2. Retro slingback in asymmetric green and white. Finished off with a rectangular block heel in vivid green. Spring/summer 2013.

3. The Damier fabric, in monochrome black and white, covers this classic pump with elongated toe and rectangular heel. Finished with a flat bow on the vamp. Spring/summer 2013.

4. Classic 1960s pump in shark-grey kid leather. A silver block heel adds a modern twist. Spring/summer 2013.

3.

Alexander Wang

Black *Marta* boot worn with the women's ready-to-wear collection for spring/summer 2013, New York Fashion Week runway show.

Influenced by French aesthetics as much as the grunge movement of the 1990s, Alexander Wang cuts the perfect balance between New York elegance and its edgier street style. Quietly innovative, his shoes combine sleek modern lines with razor-sharp detailing. Adored by his fans – and voraciously admired by his peers – Wang has achieved overnight success on a global scale, most recently having become creative director at Balenciaga, succeeding Nicolas Ghesquière.

The Alexander Wang brand philosophy is very much centred on the 'undone' and the contradiction that lies between refinement and imperfection. 'I love a chameleon – a woman who is just as seductive in t-shirt and jeans as she is in lingerie or an evening gown.'

Wang's fluid approach to design lets his ideas evolve and build naturally rather than being forced down any particular route. 'It's always a journey and we tend to keep the "box" open for exploration. I always like to let the process or character develop for itself, and then I go in and ask myself what makes this character feel like our kind of girl. I love a woman who isn't afraid to embrace her masculine side while not losing sight of her femininity; both sides are equal and often play off each other,' he explains.

His styles include feminine heels and androgynous boots and flats, with a refined leaning towards sportswear. Monochrome and muted tones play a pivotal role in Wang's collections, allowing him to focus on the materials. He juxtaposes glossy patents with matt python skin and crocodile effects, or super-smooth calf leather with ponyskin and metallic suedes. Graphic cut-outs have become

indicative of Wang's work, used with great success in his spring/summer 2013 collection.

Born and raised in San Francisco, Wang's creative calling saw him up sticks to New York at the age of 18 to study at Parsons School of Design. He went on to launch his own label in 2005, which focused primarily on knitwear. By the spring of 2007 the label had evolved into a fully-fledged women's ready-to-wear line. Footwear was to follow in 2009 alongside his 'Women's T by Alexander Wang' collection. The equivalent men's collection was launched in 2010 and his men's ready-to-wear line in 2011.

Success comes with accolades, and Wang is no exception. In 2008, at the age of 24, he won the Council of Fashion Designers of America (CFDA)/ *Vogue* Fashion Fund award and the following year the CFDA Swarovski Womenswear Designer of the Year award. In 2011 he was acknowledged by *GQ* magazine as Best Designer of the Year and by the CFDA as Best Accessory Designer.

Wang's success is evident in the 15 stores he already has worldwide. But it is a success due in part to the fact that he is realistic about his end goal: 'There always has to be a connection to the consumer and what she would actually wear on the street; that is very important to me.'

1.

2.

1. *Black Aline* T-strap sandal
   with tall slim harness strap,
   buckle closure and 11cm
   (4⅜in) geometric heel.
   Spring/summer 2013.

2. *Glacier Aline* T-strap sandal
   with tall slim harness strap
   and 11cm (4⅜in) geometric
   heel, in white calfskin.
   Spring/summer 2013.

1. *Marta* Knee-high boot in
   black calfskin with elastic
   suspension leather panelling
   and back zip closure. Spring/
   summer 2013.

1. Look book imagery of the *Jill* lace-up bootie worn with the women's ready-to-wear, resort 2013 collection.

1. *Kamila* Mary Jane bootie with cut-out panel and strap fastening, with pointed toe, topstitching and brass hardware. Fall/winter 2012/2013.

2. *Alla* An 11cm (4⅜in) wedge, in black and white embossed lizard-print leather with folded seams and contrasting heel section. Resort 2013.

3. *Jill* Black cut-out bootie with criss-cross ankle straps and 8cm (3⅛in) semi-transparent lug sole. Resort 2013.

4. *Sonja* Ankle-strap pump with pointed low-cut toe, snap closure and stiletto heel. Fall/winter 2012/2013.

Sophia Webster

Cassidy 1 Black leather strappy T-bar sandal with contrasting blue and pink buckle closures and back tassel detailing. Fall/winter 2013/2014.

Sophia Webster graduated from The Royal College of Art in 2010 and was immediately offered the position of design assistant to Nicholas Kirkwood by the designer himself, with the promise that he would help her launch her own collection after two years. She accepted this enviable opportunity and launched her own line of footwear for spring/summer 2013. She is already turning heads with her distinct and vibrant style. Her flamboyant designs take the wearer on an exhilarating journey through a kaleidoscopic world of colour, print and texture.

Choosing to follow her fashion instinct rather than seasonal trends, Webster references myriad inspirations to develop her unique style of design. For example, film director Tim Burton, C. S. Lewis's Narnia books and 1990s teen film *Clueless* are just some of the themes behind her fall/winter 2013/2014 collection 'I'm a Rainbow Too'. Not afraid to experiment, Webster will happily mix holographic leathers with leopard print, multicoloured knits, printed hearts, polka dots, metallic leathers and Perspex within the same collection. Her shoes grace many red-carpet events.

Webster's signature trademarks include single soles, feminine lines and strong silhouettes, all of which are evident in the designer's most recognizable style, the 'Riko', a high-heeled Aztec open-toe bootie.

Most of her shoes are towering delights, but she also creates flats with the same enthusiasm and vigour.

Webster's luxury footwear has a playful charm while maintaining a sophisticated elegance, a style she has been cultivating since her academic career, where she gained significant recognition including the Cordwainers at London College of Fashion Award for Excellence in 2008 followed by the Drapers Student Footwear Designer of the Year Award in 2009 and the Browns Shoe Designer Award in 2010.

Since launching her line, Webster has received the 2012 Condé Nast *Footwear News* Emerging Designer of the Year and been awarded the prestigious New Gen award for a second consecutive season by the British Fashion Council for her fall/winter 2013/2014 collection. She has launched a bag range and is stocked in some of the world's most prestigious stores; this is a designer who is fast becoming a firm favourite with fashion editors.

1.

2.

3.

1. *Amber 1* Yellow and black
   plaid pump with almond toe
   and black and white striped
   stiletto heel. Fall/winter
   2013/2014.

2. *Amis* Stiletto ankle bootie in
   iridescent holographic leather
   with black patent toe, heel,
   front strap and binding. Fall/
   winter 2013/2014.

3. *Bardot* Showstopping
   platform sandal in printed
   polka dot metallic leather
   with fuchsia-pink heel and
   straps and gold metallic
   platform. Fall/winter
   2013/2014.

1.

2.

3.

1. *Blake 2* Open-toe sandal
   with ankle tie closure and
   stiletto heel. In natural
   coloured mesh with vivid blue
   and neon-orange leopard
   appliqué. Pre-fall 2013.

2. *Emeli 1* Iridescent green
   pump with black polka dots
   and pointed toe, scalloped
   edging, floral appliqué and
   stiletto heel. Fall/winter
   2013/2014.

3. *Liza 2* Black and white polka
   dot pump with glittered
   stiletto heel and notched
   front. Fall/winter 2013/2014.

1.

2.

3.

4.

1. *Tali* Black suede peep-toe bootie with turquoise trim, mandarin-red leather stiletto heel and back lace tie closure. Pre-fall/winter 2013.

2. *Minnie 5* Black and gold polka-dot ponyskin loafer, with patent leather apron and gold bauble decoration. Fall/winter 2013/2014.

3. *Jolie 1* Over-the-knee boot with front lacing, multiple buckled strap closures and gold embroidery. Fall/winter 2013/2014.

4. *Cara 1* Pointed ankle boot with turquoise and black patent leopard-print appliqué on natural-coloured mesh and mandarin-red leather heel. Pre-fall 2013.

1.

2.

4.

3.

1. *Bardot* Metallic platform
   sandal with green and
   pink bauble on the toe
   and contrasting heel and
   platform. Fall/winter
   2013/2014.

2. *Kendall 2* Black leather ankle
   boot with fine double ankle
   straps and looped, slashed
   suede fringing. With tasselled
   back zip closure. Fall/winter
   2013/2014.

3. *Leoni 1* Holographic
   open-toe sandal with front
   teardrop cut-out, black
   floral decoration and back
   zip closure. Fall/winter
   2013/2014.

4. *Lois* Pink and blue polka-dot
   mule with black and white
   striped stiletto heel and pink
   binding. Pre-fall 2013.

Atalanta Weller

Jake A geometric cut-out ankle boot in deep tan and black. The cutaways give the illusion that the wedge heel and upper are one piece. Fall/winter 2011.

An Atalanta Weller shoe is an instantly recognizable shoe. Compelling in their innovation and architectural structure, the designs defy expected forms with their unique and avant-garde take on silhouette.

Having graduated from the famous Cordwainers College in London and gained a wealth of industry experience at Clarks, Hugo Boss and John Richmond, Weller's own-name brand was established in 2009. Her first solo collection gained her instant New Gen recognition, a design newcomer's award that she continued to win for three consecutive seasons.

The Atalanta Weller brand continues to go from strength to strength. Her designs are not just lauded on the high street and catwalk, the Victoria and Albert Museum in London recently purchased two of her designs to hold in their permanent fashion collection. Most definitely one to watch!

What inspired you to get into footwear design?
I was inspired to create beautiful aesthetic forms that also function by the great masters of the Bauhaus, while studying sculpture at art college. After a number of years gaining valuable industry experience I started experimenting with shoe forms and then collaborating with avant-garde British designers Gareth Pugh, Henry Holland and Sinha Stanic. This lead to my first collection for spring/summer 2010.

Do you have a particular kind of woman in mind when you are designing?
A modern, independent woman. I'm inspired by the women around me; women who embrace life – 'Super Women' if you like – but whose confidence is more likely to be expressed through a strong lipstick and a pair of powerful Atalanta Weller shoes than a Lycra superhero suit!

Where do you draw your inspiration from?
From many places: the buildings around me, the details of car engines, the sculpture of Jean Arp and Barbara Hepworth. Music is also a very important inspiration. The combination of the aesthetic and the technical is always a critical balance for me.

Would you say you had a signature style? Describe it to us in five words.
Sculptural graphic forms, full of subtle details.

When it comes to technique and fabric, are there particular styles and materials that run through each collection?
I love experimenting with materials, whether that means using a new synthetic Lycra, or re-evaluating well-loved Italian calf leather. I enjoy using technical materials and hidden structures to mould the shoes in subtly unusual ways.

How do you see the current fascination with footwear developing?
Shoes are fascinating; there is an amazing amount of choice out there and, as people continue to appreciate fine and beautiful shoes, there is a great opportunity to continue to develop new ideas both aesthetically and technically.

What are your ambitions for your brand in the future?
To continue to do what I love. To constantly challenge and experiment with new ideas and materials. To design great shoes for women with fluid lives who want something special and progressive that they can also love and live in.

1.

2.

4.

3.

1. *Gene* A vintage-inspired wedge sandal in a colour combination of royal and glitter blue. Buckle closure around the back of the heel. Spring/summer 2013.

2. *Wolfe* A wedge sandal with a zigzag colour-blocked pattern across the upper and sole. In royal and glitter blue combination. Spring/summer 2013.

3. *Dean* A Chelsea boot design in white leather with camel strapping around the ankle and heel. Spring/summer 2013.

4. *Arwen* An ankle bootie in nude and camel leather. Features a curved topline which sits over the ankle, and zigzag cut-out on the upper. Spring/summer 2013.

1.

2.

4.

3.

1. *Severine* Pointed ankle boot in high-shine chocolate leather. Features ankle strap closure and geometric topline. Fall/winter 2013.

2. *Suki* Dove-grey pointed T-bar with transparent plastic ankle strap and stiletto heel. Fall/winter 2013.

3. *Vivienne* Oxblood almond-toe shoe with pointed high tongue and chunky Cuban heel. Two straps in a deeper shade of red lie across the vamp. Fall/winter 2013.

4. *Solitaire* Ankle boot in soft kid leather with cutaway detail giving the illusion of a T-bar shoe, and stiletto heel. Fall/winter 2013.

Vivienne Westwood

Lilly Elevated lace-up ankle boot in red kidskin with turned-up pointed toe, as seen on the catwalk fall/winter 2013/2014.

The grande dame of British fashion, Vivienne Westwood, has created some of the world's most iconic shoes. True to her nonconformist ideals, Westwood's shoes truly break with convention and are as popular today as they were three decades ago.

Westwood first stamped her authority on the fashion world's consciousness in the mid 1970s with her shop Sex on the King's Road in London. This was the shop's third incarnation, and in 1976 she and then husband Malcolm McLaren (who managed the Sex Pistols at the time) again renamed their shop, this time Seditionaries. It was here that they played a major role in the emergence of the Punk Rock phenomenon.

By the late 1970s Westwood was already a recognized symbol of the British avant-garde. For fall/winter 1981/1982 she debuted the 'Pirates' collection from which her most iconic footwear style, the 'Pirate Boot', was born. Inspired by swashbuckling pirates, the flat androgynous-style slouchy boot featured a multitude of buckled-strap fastenings. The boot's popularity was reignited in 1999 when Kate Moss was spotted wearing an original pair. The photographer Corrine Day shot Moss in the boots for British *Vogue* around the same time, which further defined the look. Since then demand for the boots has continued.

Another famous style from the 1980s is the 'Rocking Horse Ballerina' shoe, which was created for the spring/summer 1985 'Mini-Crini' collection. This improbable shoe was designed to give poise and elevation; to put women on a pedestal, as well as create movement when worn that reflected the sway of a ballerina's tutu. It continued to play an important role in Westwood's 'Harris Tweed' collection for fall/winter 1987/88.

The 'Harris Tweed' collection marked a significant shift in direction for the queen of punk. Street culture ceased to play a major role in her work and instead she began to look to Savile Row, British fabrics such as tweed and tartan, and seventeenth- and eighteenth-century art as inspiration.

Westwood has created many legendary styles of footwear since this time. The 'Toile Print Boot' designed in 1996 was inspired by the famous sixteenth-century blue and white Dutch delftware, and her 'Trompe l'Oeil' boot was an ode to Victorian dandyism. Her 'Erotic Zones' collection of 1995 introduced the 'Mary Jane Spoon' shoe with its 15.5cm (6in) killer heel, while the British-colonial-inspired 'Sahara Plimsoll' of 1999 was an ankle-high lace-up shoe in cream canvas with strips of tan suede. No one can forget the towering 'Mock-Croc Super Elevated Ghillie' platform from which Naomi Campbell famously fell off while modelling the fall/winter 1993/1994 'Anglomania' collection.

Today Westwood's shoes have the same relevance and playful characteristics as her archive pieces. She creates without adhering to seasonal trends, choosing instead to follow her own unique vision. Her shoes will always be coveted and collected.

1. *Elevated Regent Sandal Tea Garden* Limited-edition tea garden-print platform. Vivienne Westwood 'Gold Label' collection, spring/summer 2013.

2. *Squiggle Print* Red and white printed platform boot with buckled strap detailing. 'Gold Label' collection, spring/summer 2013.

3. *Black Dear Skin* Mary Jane platform with triple-strap detailing and stiletto heel. 'Anglomania' collection, spring/summer 2013.

1.

2.

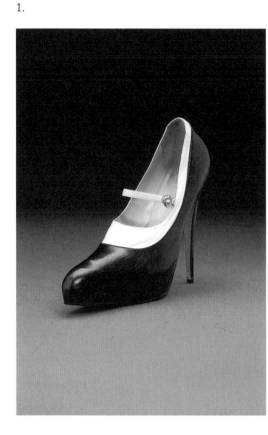

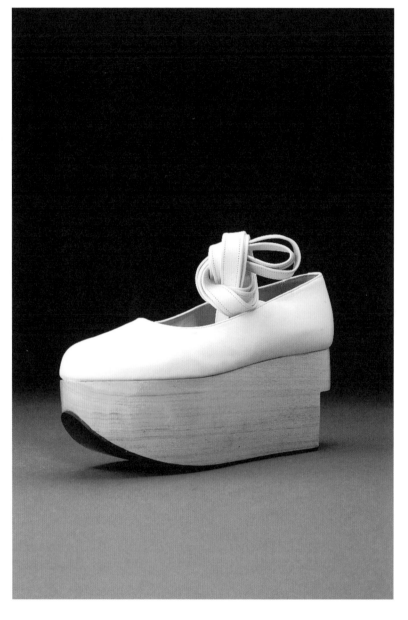

1. *Mary Jane Spoon* Two-tone
   Mary Jane with elongated
   toe and stiletto heel. 'Erotic
   Zones' collection, spring/
   summer 1995.

2. *Rocking Horse Ballerina*
   Wooden platform ballerina
   with ankle wrap ties. 'Harris
   Tweed' collection, fall/winter
   1987/1988.

1. *Lilly* Elevated lace-up ankle boot in red kidskin with pointed turned-up toe and flared leather-covered heel. Fall/winter 2013/2014.

1.

1. *Darlene* Elevated tan leather pump with pointed turned-up toe, flared leather-covered heel and red kidskin trim. Fall/winter 2013/2014.

2. *Gillian* Elevated tan leather Chelsea boot with pointed turned-up toe and flared leather-covered heel. Fall/winter 2013/2014.

3. *Charis* Kidskin ankle boot with long-hair fur trim. Fall/winter 2013/2014.

2.

3.

Picture Credits

Page 2 courtesy Jerome C. Rousseau, photographer Mary Rozzi; page 8 top courtesy Minna Parikka, bottom shoes by Anastasia Radevich, photographer Nikolas Yur; page 9 top courtesy Alexander Wang, bottom courtesy FINSK, photographer Elina Simonen; page 10 photograph by Ida Riveros; pages 12–13 courtesy Paul Andrew; pages 14–17 courtesy Aperlaï, photograph page 14 by Emmanuel Lafay; pages 18–21 courtesy Bionda Castana, spring/summer 2012 imagery photographer Aaron Tilley, creative director Natalia Barbieri, stylist Jessica Walsh, prop stylist Annette Masterman, prop stylist assistant Chloe Waller, model Izzy Schimek; pages 22–27 courtesy Edmundo Castillo; page 28 © Catwalking.com; pages 30–33 courtesy Chanel; page 34 © Rex Features Ltd; pages 36–39 courtesy Jimmy Choo, all original sketches provided by Jimmy Choo Ltd; pages 40–43 courtesy Charline de Luca; pages 44–49 courtesy DKNY, Cinemagraphs/Trunk Archive; pages 50–53 courtesy Liam Fahy, www.liamfahy.com; pages 54–57 pictures courtesy of Feminine & Masculine; pages 58–63 courtesy FINSK, page 58 photograph Elina Simonen, pages 60–63 photographs Aleksi Niemela; pages 64–69 courtesy Pedro García; page 70 © The Condé Nast Collection; pages 72–75 courtesy Pierre Hardy; page 76 © Catwalking.com; pages 78–81 courtesy Marc Jacobs; pages 82–87 courtesy Nicholas Kirkwood; pages 88–93 courtesy Zoe Lee; pages 94–97 courtesy Kat Maconie; page 98 © Catwalking.com; pages 100–103 courtesy Marni; pages 104–107 courtesy Marsèll, photography by Mirki Rizzi; pages 108–113 courtesy Daniele Michetti; pages 114–117 courtesy Chie Mihara; page 118 Fairchild Photo Service; pages 120–123 courtesy Miu Miu; pages 124–129 images provided by Chrissie Morris Ltd, page 124 photographed by Kira Lillie; pages 130–135 courtesy Charlotte Olympia; pages 136–141 courtesy Minna Parikka; page 142 © Mina Angela; page 144 courtesy Michel Perry; pages 145–147 © Laetitia Hotte; pages 148–153 courtesy Pollini; page 154 © Catwalking.com; pages 156–159 courtesy Prada; page 160 © Catwalking.com; pages 162–163 courtesy Alain Quilici, www.alainquilici.com, info@ alainquilici.com; pages 164–169 shoes designed by Anastasia Radevich, photographer Nikolas Yur; pages 170–174 courtesy Eugène Riconneaus, drawings by Eugène Riconneaus; pages 174–179 courtesy Jerome C. Rousseau, page 179 photography © Gianfilippo De Rossi; pages 180–185 shoes designed by Rupert Sanderson/ pages 180 and 185, photographer Kate Bellm, stylist Matilda Goad; pages 186–191 photos and styling by Camilla Skovgaard; pages 192–195 courtesy LD Tuttle, all photography by Zen Sekizawa; page 196 © Catwalking.com; pages 198–201 courtesy Louis Vuitton; pages 202–207 courtesy Alexander Wang; pages 208–213 courtesy Sophia Webster; pages 214–217 courtesy Atalanta Weller; page 218 © Catwalking.com; pages 220–221 courtesy Vivienne Westwood; pages 222–223 © GoRunway.com.